THE PROFESSIONAL ACTOR'S HANDBOOK

THE PROFESSIONAL ACTOR'S HANDBOOK

From Casting Call to Curtain Call

Julio Agustin
with
Kathleen Potts

ROWMAN & LITTLEFIELD PUBLISHERS, INC.
Lanham • Boulder • New York • London

Published by Rowman & Littlefield
A wholly owned subsidiary of The Rowman & Littlefield Publishing Group, Inc.
4501 Forbes Boulevard, Suite 200, Lanham, Maryland 20706
www.rowman.com

Unit A, Whitacre Mews, 26-34 Stannary Street, London SE11 4AB

British Library Cataloguing in Publication Information Available

Library of Congress Cataloging-in-Publication Data

Names: Agustin, Julio, 1967– author. | Potts, Kathleen, 1963– author.
Title: The professional actor's handbook : from casting call to curtain call
    / Julio Agustin with Kathleen Potts.
Description: Lanham, Maryland : Rowman & Littlefield, [2017] | Includes
    bibliographical references and index.
Identifiers: LCCN 2016039444 (print) | LCCN 2016055441 (ebook) | ISBN
    9781442277717 (hardback : alk. paper) | ISBN 9781442277724 (pbk. : alk.
    paper) | ISBN 9781442277731 (electronic)
Subjects: LCSH: Acting—Handbooks, manuals, etc.
Classification: LCC PN2061 .A48 2017 (print) | LCC PN2061 (ebook) | DDC
    792.02/8—dc23
LC record available at https://lccn.loc.gov/2016039444

∞™ The paper used in this publication meets the minimum requirements of American National Standard for Information Sciences—Permanence of Paper for Printed Library Materials, ANSI/NISO Z39.48-1992.

Printed in the United States of America

To my Pop, my real-life superhero who continues to inspire me, and to my late husband, Glenn, who continues to watch over me.

Finally, to the students in the Transition Workshop everywhere who helped to shape the strategies in this book. Looks like we made it!

—Julio

To my parents, who instilled in me a strong work ethic, the power of perseverance, and a willingness to serve others for the "greater good."

—Kathleen

Contents

Foreword

Elizabeth Parkinson

I MET JULIO AGUSTIN AS a performer in my first Broadway show, *Fosse*. Julio is a striking presence onstage, a gifted actor and singer, and a wonderful dancer. Imagine my surprise years later when I was asked to join the faculty of the new musical theatre program at Western Connecticut State University and learned that the supervisor of the new program was none other than Julio Agustin! It was a pleasure to reconnect in a university setting away from the pressures of Broadway, auditioning, and finding our next job. At WestConn, Julio was a wonderful mentor to me, teaching me so much about guiding students, university education, and career development for our undergraduates. I was impressed with Julio's knowledge and his commitment to helping actors realize their goals in a straightforward and honest way through his teaching and his Transition Workshops.

The first thought that came to mind after reading *The Professional Actor's Handbook: From Casting Call to Curtain Call* was "Where was this book when I needed it?" The second thought was "I am purchasing this for my husband, Broadway veteran Scott Wise, who is reentering the business after a ten-year hiatus!"

This handbook by Julio Agustin with Kathleen Potts is one of the most comprehensive books I have seen for performers entering or already active in the field. After reading it, I felt inspired. I am already working to update my own "unique selling points"! Many of the tactics I learned are applicable to any career. Artists spend so much time honing their craft, but there is very little education dedicated to the nuts and bolts of pursuing a performance career. Many actors enter the business only to become discouraged.

Many move on to other careers. I appreciate the positive narrative that Julio and Kathleen put forth and the proactive steps for organizing your career. Julio guides us to finding the love and the art in the process. He encourages a sense of creativity rather than drudgery when nurturing one's career.

On top of it all, Julio's warm and witty personality makes an appearance with stories gleaned from his own experiences. The advice never seems preachy; rather, it is comforting to know that he has experienced the ups and downs of the career of which he speaks.

I have also seen the results of Julio's coaching in many of my own students. The Transition Workshop gets results, and I am thrilled that this information is available now in *The Professional Actor's Handbook: From Casting Call to Curtain Call* by Julio Agustin with Kathleen Potts. It should be required reading for all actors, singers, and dancers who are pursuing a professional career, and I highly recommend it for professionals in the field who are looking to jump-start or reinvigorate their careers.

Multifaceted and highly awarded, Elizabeth Parkinson has received nominations for Best Actress in a Musical (Tony Award) and Best Featured Actress in a Musical (Outer Critics Circle and Drama Desk Awards). She is also winner of the highly coveted Astaire Award for Best Female Dancer on Broadway and a Master Teacher of dance and musical theatre performance. Elizabeth Parkinson is currently the artistic director of FineLine Theatre Arts in New Milford, CT; Artists in Motion youth ballet company; and Vineyard Arts Project Musical Theatre Lab.

Acknowledgments

I TEND TO BE ONE OF THOSE people who miss what is right in front of his nose. If I neglect to acknowledge you in this section, please feel free to bop me in the head the next time you see me!

Special thanks go to my life coach, Dr. Anthony Gaudioso; my almost-illustrator, Dhafir Jackson; friends and family who have pushed me (including Derrick, Kava, Bonnie, Jeffrey, Kathleen, Tiffany and Alexander, Monica and Andrzej, the Spadaro family for all of their love and support, and agents Barry and Jeb); my family (Pop, Ma, sisters, and cousins); my mentors, Sharron "Mrs. Roberts" Hughes, Suzanne, Kate, and Gayle (go FSU!); my original superhero, Jonathan Flom; my students, who have also been my teachers; my clients, who have helped me to develop, refine, and test my Top Fifteen Transition Strategies; Stephen Ryan and the team at Rowman and Littlefield; my longtime friend and accountant Ruth Beltran; my colleagues at various universities, including Joan Melton and Jennie Morton of the One-Voice Institute for the Integration of Voice and Movement, John Franceschina (mentor and collaborator, *Out of Line*); my extended Broadway family (Elizabeth, Scott, Jerry, Janelle, Andy, Rosa, Stro, Chita, Jerry, Kurt—too many to name); Dr. John P. McCarty for making me smile again; and of course my cowriter, Dr. Kathleen Potts, without whom this book would not have been possible.

—Julio

Special thanks to my mentors: Dr. Melvin Howards, Dr. David Paul Willinger, and Gertrude Stewart Warnock. Gratitude to my teachers from grade school to grad school; you have been influential in infinitesimal ways: Mrs. H., Miss Trax, Mr. Pleasure, "Ma" Hurley, Sarah Franklin, Power and Steele, Eduardo Machado, Dr. Arnold Aronson, Anne Bogart, Tom Gilmore, Beth Henley, Tina Howe, Kristin Linklater, Evangeline Morphos, Keith Reddin, Mr. Gerald Schoenfeld, Kelly Stuart, Robert Woodruff, Dr. Marvin Carlson, Dr. Dan Gerould, Dr. Jean Graham-Jones, and Dr. David Savran. Kudos to my fellow educators: Brandon, David, Peggy, Rob, Jen and Jen, and Tara (and Randy, too). Thanks, thanks, thanks for life lessons learned from Julia Tiffany, Duane, Rusty, M. and M., the Nelson clan, Kimberly and Jason Ramírez, and Jenny K. and family. Words always seem sufficient, except when describing the things I am grateful for in Julio Agustin.

—Kathleen

Introduction

You've got talent. You *know* this. Now you're looking for an edge to move ahead in the business. You've already spent years training and reading a lot of great theatre books, and now you spot this one: *The Professional Actor's Handbook: From Casting Call to Curtain Call*. What's different about this book? This is actually a *workbook*: a book about *work*. It is not about following your dreams—the world is full of unemployed dreamers. *The Professional Actor's Handbook* is about taking action, about *doing* the things that will guarantee that your dreams become a reality. Dreams are about the future, but this book is about the present, about *doing something right now!*

The seventeen success strategies found in *The Professional Actor's Handbook* have been improving the success rate for actors, singers, dancers, and the triple-threat musical theatre performers of Broadway for more than fifteen years. They are field-tested, tried-and-true techniques that have helped performers to establish themselves as working professionals in the industry. The success strategies will change the way you live, work, and create your overall future, helping you to build a steady career in the performing arts.

This book is divided into four sections: part I, "Branding Strategies for the Professional Actor"; part II, "Success Strategies for the Stage and Screen"; part III, "Marketing and Networking Strategies for the Successful Performer"; and part IV, "Offstage and Professionalization Strategies." It is highly recommended that you begin with part I because branding is the key to a twenty-first-century acting career, whether it is onstage, online, or even on reality TV. Once you are crystal clear as to what it is that you are selling (i.e., *your brand*), you can follow this by reading the book straight through or skipping around to whichever chapters fill your need or capture your attention.

Part II offers up "Success Strategies for the Stage and Screen": "Create a Captivating Resume," "Take That 'Perfect' Headshot," "Write a Standout Cover Letter," and "Compile a Complete Rep Book." We complete this section by sharing the secrets to the successful audition with "Practice Preparation" and "Conquer Audition Nerves."

Part III, "Marketing and Networking Strategies for the Successful Performer," will help you to land that breakout role. Living and working in the twenty-first century requires a presence on social media; therefore, generating a marketing plan that utilizes social media tools is essential for today's working professional. In addition to marketing, success strategy 10 helps to keep you healthy, happy, and motivated by establishing your team. Success strategy 11 focuses on the need to connect yourself to a mentor in the industry and includes a must-read interview with Los Angeles television casting director Jeffrey Drew. At this point, directors may want to follow the casting director's advice and hire you, but you will need success strategy 12 to learn how to get them to trust you. And finally, in success strategies 13 and 14, we give you the 411 on networking and following up for superior results.

The final section covers "Offstage and Professionalization Strategies," but it could have as easily been titled "Show Me the Money!" Its first strategy guides the working actor on how to set up your personal workspace, prepare the "go-bag" for auditions, and get a handle on managing your basic finances. Success strategy 16 guides you through the maze of landing the perfect survival job that will support your performance career. To conclude, now that you have gotten that first job offer, it is time to negotiate. Have no fear; we walk you through a simple, step-by-step formula for negotiating and getting the most out of the contract. Boom! You're done. Sign on the dotted line, and look forward to taking your bow!

It doesn't matter whether you've encountered *The Professional Actor's Handbook: From Casting Call to Curtain Call* as a text in a college or university class or as a supplement to the Transition Workshop Studio in New York City or walked into a bookshop and saw it on a shelf or been gifted it by a friend or ordered it online; the important thing is that you've now got the tools for success in your hands. It's time for you to take action and establish your career as a *working* professional.

Part I

BRANDING STRATEGIES FOR THE PROFESSIONAL ACTOR

Success Strategy 1

Define Your Unique Selling Points

WHY DO THEY HIRE YOU instead of all of the other talented, beautiful, amazing "yous" in the audition waiting room? It is because of the unique value that you bring to this industry and, more important, to the project for which you are auditioning. They choose *you* because they are able to clearly see "it" in you, because you clearly possess something different from everyone else who has come before or after you.

By defining your brand with clear and compelling unique selling points (USPs), you will be leaps and bounds ahead of those who believe that this industry is really casting someone who can do it all! The *unique selling proposition* is a term developed by Rosser Reeves as a marketing strategy for advertising campaigns in the 1940s; we apply a very similar strategy here to market you. Understand that nobody can do it all, not in the ninety seconds that they give you in the audition room. Therefore, it is of the utmost importance that you separate yourself by clearly defining what it is that you are marketing—the best you.

Your actor USPs are composed of three words. Selecting the perfect three words takes some time and effort (as well as a little back-and-forth with a thesaurus). Yet once you have selected the best USPs for yourself, not only is your work easier and more focused, but also you can finally begin to enter showbiz with confidence, knowing that you are maximizing your audition strategies and marketing a clear brand in your career. These three words influence everything that you do, from the audition pieces you perform to the clothing you wear to the headshot you select and many other aspects of your profession.

I recall conducting a workshop with Broadway casting director Arnold Mungioli in which he stated that, no matter how nervous an actor might be during the audition process, those behind the table (producers, directors, casting directors, and playwrights) are ten times as nervous as you are. These people have invested countless months (or even years) and perhaps millions of dollars in that one particular project. For example, the Tony Award–winning musical *Fosse* had been in the works for more than ten years and underwent several Equity and out-of-town productions before finally coming to Broadway. The amount of time, money, and bold changes that were made to get the project "just right" and worthy of a Broadway audience would astound anyone.

My hope is that this information excites you rather than puts more pressure on you. Given this knowledge, do you really believe that "they" want you to fail during your audition? Do you really think that they "have it in for you," that they are thinking negative thoughts about you during your monologue performance or rendition of your song? Of course not! Many actors actually believe this, yet they couldn't be further from the truth. Imagine the people behind the table having a conversation right before you come in about wishing that someone with all of your qualities and talent would walk through the door and show them what they've been waiting for all day. Directors and their teams want you to be amazing and fabulous; they need you to be the answer to their prayers!

Once you can come to terms with this, your perspective switches from a pessimistic "trying to get the job" to an enthusiastic showcasing of your talents, skills, and personality—of all that you have to offer—with confidence. Your thought process will now go something like this: "I am the answer to all of your problems—look no further, I have arrived!" In fact, if you are not thinking this, then you really are wasting your time. If you don't believe that you are "the one," then how in the heck are they going to believe this?

But what does it mean to be "the one," and how do you define this in a way that guarantees results? To find the answer to this, I find it helpful to look to corporate America and how successful businesses go about marketing their unique products in a competitive world. How do business executives define success when it comes to marketing a specific product? (And let's face it, you are a commodity that needs to be marketed!) One business strategy is to define what is known as the product's unique selling proposition (adapted into a set of unique selling points, or USPs, for this book).

In his book *Reality in Advertising*, Rosser Reeves suggests that a product (in our case, the actor or performer) advertises itself in three ways, by

1. Clearly displaying its qualities
2. Offering a unique benefit not offered by the competition
3. Attracting new customers

In Rosser's assessment, the product's unique selling proposition includes those characteristics that allow one product to stand out from a group of similar products. For example, what is it about Starbucks that has allowed it to become a multimillion-dollar company with franchises and worldwide appeal? Is it quality (authentic organic Arabica beans from South America, the original maker of coffee beans)? Is it customization (unlike the other "fast-coffee" houses, each product at Starbucks is not only created to order on the spot with speed and precision and to the specificity of the buyer or consumer but also is of the highest quality and specificity of the consumer)? Or is it style (a comfortable, relaxed setting with a friendly atmosphere conducive to lounging, working, or meeting friends and work partners)? Perhaps the answer is not specifically any one of these but rather the perfect combination of all of these—quality, customization, and style—that has allowed Starbucks to quickly evolve into a successful and trustworthy business that is easily recognized by the little green logo. Pretty simple concept, don't you think?

Similarly, you must define what it is that makes you an original, a quality performer, someone with just the right style, to sufficiently impress the auditors to the point that you earn a callback. This perfect combination equals your USPs!

Because we are not cups of coffee but actors and performers, I have managed to translate the trio of adjectives from "quality, customization, and style" to more appropriately coincide with those qualities that most directors and producers are seeking. After several years of trial and error, I have narrowed these three adjectives to the following: reputation, type, and personality.

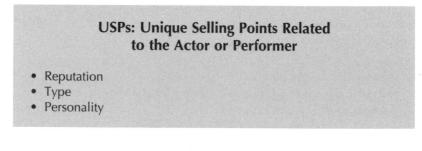

USPs: Unique Selling Points Related to the Actor or Performer

- Reputation
- Type
- Personality

I have discovered, through my years of performing on Broadway and now coaching others, that just the right combination of these three allows producers, directors, and casting directors to see the *talent* (that's *you*) as clearly and as specifically as possible. This helps them immensely, thereby allowing them to do their job much more efficiently; and believe me, they will love you for making their jobs easier!

DISCOVERING YOUR ACTOR USPS

The following are detailed definitions for each of the USPs for reputation, type, and personality. Your challenge now is to spend some quiet time working to define each of these for yourself. It is imperative that you choose one word or phrase—the perfect, juiciest word or phrase—for each of the three categories. I recommend that you use a thesaurus in order to maximize your success.

Describe Your Reputation

Ours is an industry in which your reputation precedes you. You may not yet believe this, but people will hear and know about you and your work before you have actually begun to work steadily in the industry. There's no getting around this; it's the nature of our business.

With that said, what is it about you that would allow the auditors to trust you with their valuable project? What is it about your work ethic that makes you stand out from the crowd? Are you reliable? Or are you a detailed worker? Are you committed? Is it your ability to be trustworthy that stands out to employers? Or are you a flexible human being, able to go with the flow? Maybe you are able to multitask (great qualities of understudies and swings).

An example is screen actor Matthew McConaughey and his reputation for being extremely committed to his roles. Everyone knows that he is someone who enjoys throwing himself into each role, sometimes bulking up to play a stripper (*Magic Mike*) or losing fifty pounds to portray a victim of the AIDS epidemic (*Dallas Buyers Club*). *Committed* is a perfect word for someone who would go to such extremes to convincingly portray a character.

You might consider asking those for whom you have worked in the past what it was that made them hire (or rehire) you. Choose the one word that most closely defines your reputation or work ethic.

Adjectives for Reputation

Accomplished • Adaptable • Ambitious • Analytical • Assertive • Audacious • Cheerleader • Committed • Conscientious • Consistent • Creative • Credentialed • Dependable • Determined • Diligent • Diplomatic • Direct • Down to Earth • Efficient • Energetic • Enterprising • Enthusiastic • Flexible • Focused • Genuine • Honest • Imaginative • Independent • Intellectual • Intense • Knowledgeable • Leader • Logical • Loyal • Methodical • Motivated • Open-Minded • Optimistic • Organized • Outgoing • Patient • Perceptive • Pleasant • Polite • Positive • Powerful • Practical • Productive • Professional • Realistic • Regal • Reliable • Resourceful • Respectful • Responsible • Self-Reliant • Sensible • Sincere • Solid • Solution-Oriented • Sophisticated • Stable • Strong • Successful • Tactful • Team Player • Thoughtful • Traditional • Trustworthy • Unconventional • Upbeat • Vibrant

Describe Your Type as an Actor or Performer

Here you want to describe the type(s) of roles for which you seem to be most suited. This can feel limiting, and it is, but for very good reasons.

I had a very good friend who moved to Los Angeles to work and did not want to be limited by anyone. He professed to being a legitimately trained actor (and he was) and therefore felt that he could play a multitude of roles. But the truth is that he didn't work for years, and it is my not-so-humble opinion that it was because he wasn't willing to accept that he, too, was a type. However, he has since created a steady stream of successful gigs and has a career as a working actor, in part due to his renewed strategy of marketing a specific type to industry professionals. In fact, he is one of the first people that casting directors think of for certain roles because of his ability to create a specific brand!

The goal for the actor should not be to get hired for his or her ability to play every role but for the ability to play one particular role "better" than anyone else auditioning for the role. It has been my experience that you get hired for being a specific type, but you get rehired for being talented! Isn't this, in many ways, freeing for you? Don't try to display your versatility at the very beginning; instead, focus on one particular type of role, the kind that you can play better than anyone out there. And once you book that one role, prove to them through your actions, behavior, and work ethic that you are a trained, skilled, dependable, and talented person whom they can consider for a multitude of future roles. And this, my friends, is show *business*! Once my students and clients understand and accept this, their careers are propelled forward in a way that they never imagined. It's a formula that works, so play with it, and enjoy the results!

So what's your type? Can you think of an actor or actress that exudes a certain type? What comes to mind when you think of Neil Patrick Harris? Is he, perhaps, a quirky leading man? How about Amy Sedaris? Is she outrageously comedic? Type is not only what we see when you walk into a room but also the essence that you exude and the "scent" that you leave once you exit the audition studio. For example, are you risky, edgy, quirky, versatile, outlandishly comedic, brooding, or misunderstood? Think beyond the traditional "girl next door" to a more specific and interesting "girl next door with more than meets the eye" (Jennifer Aniston has this market cornered). Or perhaps the type of "best friend" could become "nerdy best friend" (e.g., Mayim Bialik). Be specific, clear, and concise in selecting your word or phrase.

Another tip to help clarify your type is to take a look at the roles on your resume to see how others have cast you. Warning: It isn't how you see yourself (which, unfortunately, nobody cares about) but how others see you even before you open up your mouth to say a word or sing a note. Do not fall into the trap of trying to squeeze yourself into something that you want to play rather than something that is an obvious type for you to play. This is a difficult thing for many, especially young actors, to understand and accept. Just remember that type is about getting you in the door; once you're in, you can show them your skill and versatility. But you must first accept that no one is looking for versatile when casting a type; they are looking to fill a role, and type is how they fill it!

Typing is categorizing; we do this in real life, and theatre is often about portraying real life. As an extra step, you may wish to make a list of your dream roles and deduce the quality that is most prominent in each these parts. Once you get started, it will blow your mind how clear you can be by defining your type or essence. Have fun with this!

Sample USP Types

- Comedic ingénue
- Sassy best friend
- Misunderstood blue-collar worker
- Classic leading lady
- Edgy boy next door
- Sensual leading man
- Nerdy character actor
- Quirky country bumpkin
- Athlete or jock
- Urban intellectual
- Smarmy hipster
- Bubbly airhead

The list is endless!

For television, depending on experience, you may be a series regular, recurring role, guest star, costar, or under 5. For film roles, types include lead, supporting, principal, and featured.

Describe Your Most Appealing Personality Trait

What is it about you, the nonindustry you, that real-human-being you, that is going to make directors want to call you back and eventually work with you?

Back in the day, there was a saying that (the mostly male) directors hire men that they want to have a beer with and women that they want to sleep with! This, of course, is a politically incorrect statement that is rarely said out loud today, which makes me think that there is probably still some truth to it!

Yet without taking the statement too seriously, what is it about you that directors find attractive and want to be around for nine hours a day, six days a week? Are you sassy, charming, intriguing, fabulous, a jokester, grounded, good natured, down to earth, optimistic, silly, a guy's guy, or just plain nice? Again, it might be helpful to ask your friends why they choose to hang out with you. But be warned: They might just tell you the truth, so make sure that you're ready to hear it!

Sample USP Personality Traits

- Witty
- Enthusiastic
- Cheerleader
- Nurturing
- Optimistic
- Grounded
- Approachable
- Sentimental

And again, the list is endless.

Congratulations! You have now created your perfect trilogy of adjectives, your reputation, type, and personality—your USPs! Memorize and carry these words with you everywhere you go. These three simple words, adjectives to describe *you*, can now be taken into consideration for everything from writing your resume to picking just the right headshot to selecting the perfect audition outfit, monologue, song, and so on. Make sure that you can truly embody this brand, as we continue to implement it throughout this book. The USPs must be considered in everything you do in order for all of the pieces to fall into place.

─────────────────○─────────────────

Build Your Brand by Following the Stars

IN THIS CHAPTER, we explore two very different and powerful methods for maximizing your brand and expanding its impact. Unlike typical marketing strategies, however, where the advertising company might seek to let the buyers know about the product by describing it for its own merits (e.g., what it does that is so unique or how it is different from the competition), our branding strategy may seem offbeat and extremely unconventional, but it gets phenomenal results.

MAKING YOUR BRAND RELATABLE

In this, our second part of defining your unique selling points, the aim is to take your brand and *relate it to those who have come before you,* especially those who are either currently working professionals or are memorable artists who have made an impact on the industry. In other words, in order to research existing material that supports your brand, success strategy 2 instructs you to list the names, faces, and fame of well-known actors/performers from every performing-arts venue (stage, television, film, commercials, commercial print, voice-overs) and promote yourself as the next *insert-name-of-performing-artist-here.*

I know that this is where I may lose many of my readers, at least temporarily. I understand that all your life you were told how special you really are. Perhaps since birth or grade school but surely in the four years that you were in undergraduate school or the three years you spent in grad school or with your private acting coach or voice teacher, you focused on honing your technical skills and those traits and abilities that are unique so as to market your own *unique* brand.

But what I am now insisting to you is that you focus on how utterly un-unique you are and find ways to compare yourself to others who have come before you and have made a mark on the industry. Don't worry—we definitely come back to what makes you special (we actors do love to talk about ourselves, don't we?), but for now, let us focus on someone who is *like* you but not you.

You have to trust me here; being able to articulate how you remind others of this person, this current and relevant actor, this well-respected and hugely impactful artist, is our first goal. By the way, it is also a highly regarded skill that is looked for and valued by today's working agents and casting directors. Let us say that, for example, you are a five-foot blond, a comedic coloratura, who walks into the audition studio, sings a lovely yet generic song, and then leaves the audition studio. After ten hours of listening to one good singer after another, the likelihood of that actress earning a callback is extremely low.

However, let us say that you are still that five-foot blond, comedic coloratura, who walks into the audition studio, glamorously dressed with four-inch heels and slightly tamed pageant hair, and you crack a joke in your introduction that is immediately followed by a glorious rendition of "Glitter and Be Gay" from *Candide* or a sophisticated "Gorgeous" from *The Apple Tree* or a compelling and unpredictable "Never" from *On the Twentieth Century*. Who does this remind you of? Yes, you have succeeded in reminding the auditors of the incredibly talented and preciously comedic Kristin Chenoweth; hence, by clearly strategizing your audition so as to help the auditors to type you, you have done your job. And hopefully the production calls for a Kristin Chenoweth type; if so, then you, my friend, are now safely in the running!

Of course, you are not Kristin Chenoweth, nor is it your aim to be Kristin Chenoweth. You are you, and thankfully, there is no other person in the world like you, nor will there ever be. But in the work of branding, your number-one job is exactly that: to remind people of an existing product that has previously served them in some way, either by giving them joy and satisfying their taste buds, conquering their need for speed, pacifying their uncontrollable addiction, or satiating whatever that need may be before they will feel comfortable "settling" for you.

The high school athlete in need of basketball sneakers is often in search of the Nike Kobe, the LeBron, or the highly coveted Air Jordans when seeking to make a sneaker purchase. To the youngster, these sneakers represent quality, value, and, perhaps most especially, prestige. However, considering that mom is tagging along and footing the bill, ultimately the teenager opts for a pair of similarly colored and edgy high-tops with the neon laces and steady traction that are made by a generic brand and sold at the local Payless Shoe Store for the unbelievably discounted price of fifteen dollars! Not quite the prestige that he wanted but all of the other characteristics.

I attended a business workshop a few years ago in which the facilitator spoke regarding the science behind logo recognition. According to this speaker, such logo samples as the Nike swoosh or the shapes and colors of the Pepsi-Cola tricolored circle were presented to people unfamiliar with the brand; it took exactly seven exposures of the visual logo for a consumer to feel that the product was trustworthy. In other words, it wasn't until the consumer saw the logo seven times that they began to equate it with other similar products and eventually trust it to fulfill the task.

Imagine trusting your hair to just any person with a pair of scissors or your coffee from any regular corner salesman. Most of us spend a lot of time and research (even if that research is recommendations from friends) before getting a haircut or buying a cup of coffee. Why on earth, then, do we expect that a Broadway producer is going to entrust her multimillion-dollar project to just any actor, singer, or dancer? Now does this make sense?

Until you have created your own recognizable and trustworthy brand that others feel comfortable referring to each other, it is essential to create a marketing strategy that is supplemented with an essence of another relevant and recognizable working professional. For example, let us say that you have been told that you are super funny and have pretty but quirky looks and a memorable voice. Even say that you have been told that you remind people of Stephanie Courtney, perhaps better known as Flo from the Progressive commercials. Flo is often seen in such situations as getting burned at the stake, à la Joan of Arc, or singing the praises of the company, always with a tongue-in-cheek sort of wit.

Also consider Melanie Paxson, another brunette comedic actress who is perhaps better known for her witty quips in the Yoplait, Fiber One, and Serta iComfort Sleep System commercials. If you are of a similar type and have the training and skill to do this type of work, then providing a hint of these ladies at an audition at the right time will propel you roads ahead of those auditioning before and after you who are also seeking a callback. So to be clear, the first part of our marketing strategy is to remind the auditors of someone that they have seen before and with whom they are comfortable.

GETTING THE AUDITORS TO TRUST YOU

Part 2 of this second USPs marketing strategy is to get the auditors to trust you by *auditioning with material by other successful artists who have come before you.* It is not uncommon for actors to leave the audition studio while the auditors mention to each other "that actor reminds me of so-and-so." This, my friends, is almost always a very good sign. By selecting well-written material by those who have come before you—recognizable people from the stage, television, film, or successful ad campaigns whose career you wouldn't mind emulating—you will help make the auditor's job a breeze.

Depending on the amount of time that the performer wishes to dedicate to this aspect of her work, there are several ways to do this. A good vocal, monologue, or audition coach will actually do this work for you. However, it is still essential for the informed artist to know the work of those whose career they are in the market of taking over. On a very positive note, I have found that many of today's young people are very up to date in the more recent movies, plays, and musicals and have oftentimes already done much of this work; they just didn't know that they were doing it!

Complete this sentence: "I am the next _____!"

EXPANDING YOUR OPTIONS THROUGH RESEARCH

Begin by researching working professionals who have come before you whose career you believe that you can emulate. You can also state it as "I am a young _____" (only make sure that person is not in the audition room when you say it). Almost every working professional eventually has to turn down work that is offered to them; they cannot say yes to every project. Therefore, "I am available to play anything that _____ cannot take on due to scheduling" is a fun way of seeing the reality of the casting process and how reminding the auditors that you are equally talented and available. This greatly increases your odds of solidifying your career as a working professional.

Let us say that, for example, you are a twenty-something young lady who usually auditions for dramatic roles that are edgy with a misunderstood personality. If you are a belter with a high mix and are taller than 5'4", then you might start by looking at what you currently have in your audition book that has worked for you. Let's say that you have "Defying Gravity" from the Stephen Schwartz musical *Wicked* as your contemporary dramatic piece. You could then continue your material research by seeking information on the original performer, in this case, Idina Menzel (see table 2.1).

This information is used to explore additional material that is fitting for someone of your type and abilities. In searching for additional pieces, you might first look into the musical for additional songs. In this case, Elphaba sings two additional songs worth knowing, "I'm Not That Girl," a contemporary ballad, and "No Good Deed," a contemporary dramatic piece. Given this information, you might consider one of these to fill the holes in your book or to replace another song that might not be working as well as you would like.

Next, you might research the composer, Stephen Schwartz, and in doing so would discover that he has written several musicals with strong young female roles that you could play, including *Godspell*, *Pippin*, *The Magic Show*, *The Baker's Wife*, *Rags*, and *Children of Eden*. You would follow this by looking for roles within these shows that support your "edgy and misunderstood dramatic high-mixer" type. Perhaps one role would be Catherine from *Pippin*. Eve from *Children of Eden* would also support this search. Cal from *The Magic Show* or Genevieve from *The Baker's Wife* might work as well.

Ta-da! Just from this little bit of research, you have increased your knowledge of roles in the genre fourfold. Further investigation would, once again, help you to decide if "Defying Gravity" is the best song for your rep or if it wouldn't be "Kind of Woman," "I Guess I'll Miss the Man," "The Spark of Creation," "West End Avenue," or "Meadowlark." Isn't this exciting so far?

But wait: You're not done with the opportunities yet. The next thing that you want to research is the original performer's roles. Idina Menzel has listed in her credits the following stage roles: Maureen in *Rent*, Kate in the off-Broadway production of *The Wild Party*, Dorothy in *Summer of '42*, Sheila in *Hair*, Amneris in *Aida*, Florence in *Chess*, and Elizabeth Vaughn in *If/Then*. Having this knowledge further increases your repertoire options by providing you with the following possibilities: "Take Me or Leave Me," "Life of the Party," "Easy to Be Hard," "Good Morning, Sunshine," "I Know the Truth," "Heaven Help My Heart," and "You Learn to Live Without." Again, how's that for possibilities?

Last, in our goal to explore possible options simply based on your first piece, "Defying Gravity," I ask you to research all other actresses who have portrayed the role of Elphaba and who seem to market a similar set of USPs as you. In this list, you will find the names Shoshana Bean, Eden Espinosa, Ana Gasteyer, Julia Murney, Stephanie J. Block, Mandy Gonzalez, and Teal Wicks. That's seven new people whose careers you can begin to explore and can also use as a conversation piece during your next interview ("Sure,

Table 2.1. Expanding the Performer's Repertoire

Performer	Show	Role	Writer	Piece	Other Performers	Additional Material
Idina Menzel	Wicked	Elphaba	Stephen Schwartz	"Defying Gravity"	Shoshana Bean, Eden Espinosa, Ana Gasteyer, Julia Murney, Stephanie J. Block, Mandy Gonzalez, Teal Wicks	"I'm Not That Girl," "No Good Deed"
	Rent	Maureen	Jonathan Larson	"Over the Moon"	Annaleigh Ashford	"Take Me or Leave Me"
	The Wild Party	Kate	Andrew Lippa	"Look at Me Now"		"The Life of the Party"
	Aida	Amneris	Elton John	"My Strongest Suit"	Sherie Rene Scott, Felicia Finley	"I Know the Truth"
	Hair	Sheila	MacDermot/Rado/Ragni	"Easy to Be Hard"	Caissie Levy	"Good Morning, Sunshine"
	Pippin		Stephen Schwartz	"Kind of Woman"	Jill Clayburgh, Betty Buckley, Rachel Bay Jones	"I Guess I'll Miss the Man"
	Children of Eden	Eve	Stephen Schwartz	"The Spark of Creation"	Shezwae Powell	
	The Baker's Wife	Genevieve	Stephen Schwartz	"Meadowlark"	Alice Ripley	"Where Is the Warmth?"
	The Magic Show	Cal	Stephen Schwartz	"West End Avenue"	Dale Soules (currently on Orange Is the New Black)	"Lion Tamer"

I love the work of and feel I am the next Teal Wicks!"). Plus, if you research these powerhouse actresses, then you will find that many of them have played roles that I have already mentioned (e.g., Sheila in *Hair*, Maureen in *Rent*, and Eve in *Children of Eden*).

And that, ladies and gentlemen, is how you increase your marketability by following the stars who have come before you!

Part II

SUCCESS STRATEGIES FOR THE STAGE AND SCREEN

─────────○─────────

Create a
Captivating Resume

JUST ABOUT EVERY business-of-acting book discusses the parts of
the theatrical resume at length, often including templates of the
different parts of the resume; that is, name, contact information,
experience, training, and special skills. However, what is most often
lacking from these source books is an in-depth discussion of how to
maximize one's resume in order to make the greatest impact. This
includes strategies for identifying and clearly delineating exactly
who the performer is and what it is that they have to offer that is
different from others in their category.

As mentioned in chapter 1, the actor's unique selling points, or
USPs, are key to defining oneself in this industry. Consequently, a
clear resume that also communicates reputation, type, and personality is essential for the transitioning working professional.

The most effective resume lets people know *exactly who you
are* and *how they can use you* to the fullest extent. Acting training
aside, the resume works best when it tells the buyer (e.g., casting
director, director, or producer) not only the types of roles you can
play or have played but also the type of person you are, both in the
rehearsal studio as well as after hours. It has to showcase not only
your best credits first but also your personality and work ethic.
Given that the average time a resume is perused is two to three
seconds, it is vital that the actor showcase a clear resume that encompasses the USPs.

When coaching actors, I recommend that they do their homework by researching as many books and online resources on writing an actor resume as possible. Actors should research samples of actor resumes online for ideas on the various fonts, templates, styles, and general formatting. I advise actors to "steal" the best aspects of the resumes that they find, and I am only half-kidding in this. As already mentioned, choice in formatting and style is individual; therefore, noticing and taking on some of these ideas from online resumes is crucial to creating the most effective resume possible.

I have included here a few different professional actor resumes at various stages of their careers. These are included with each actor's permission and the knowledge that they are being considered for their specific style. You have their permission to "steal" aspects and appropriate some of these in creating or refining your own resume.

Once you have built your one-page resume, take a break; go and do something fun to celebrate that you are halfway there. Once you return from your break, you will have a fresh perspective to ensure that you have created a resume that is *specific*, *concise*, and *clear*.

STRATEGIES FOR CREATING A CAPTIVATING RESUME

Creating a Captivating Resume

1. Be specific.
2. Be concise.
3. Be clear.

Resume Strategy 1: Be Specific

Your working actor's resume must be indicative of who you are, highlight your unique and particular strengths, and demonstrate *exactly* how you should be cast. Yes, you are a trained actor who is versatile at playing many roles, but this versatility is likely not going to serve you at first. The goal to getting in the door is to showcase what you do better than anybody else (as noted in the USPs).

First and foremost, you must list your name as specifically as possible. Make sure that you are using a name that (1) is not already in use by another actor and (2) is indicative of who you are as defined by your USPs. You should also plan to contact Actors' Equity Association and Screen Actors Guild/American Federation of Television and Radio Artists (SAG/AFTRA) and ask them if there is another actor with your name already working in the union. Even if you are planning on working as a nonunion actor for a few years, you will not want to have to deal with changing your name once you decide to join the union.

If your name is already taken, as in the case of renowned actress Vanessa Williams, then you may do one of several things. You can choose to add a middle initial, or you might consider dropping a part of your name. Some viable options are to use your middle name as either a middle or last name or perhaps add a surname, such as Jr. or III, or simply just change your name altogether. Table 3.1 lists examples of name alterations that were made for various reasons yet all intended to highlight the actors' specific USPs.

Following your name, you must list specific information about yourself. If you are a trained singer with sight-reading skills, be specific in your vocal type and style, and list this underneath your name. Some examples of vocal types are lyric baritone, rock tenor with high C, mezzo-soprano with belt, and soprano with high mix. Also, if you consider yourself a musician and know how to read music, list your vocal range under your name. This item of specificity will tell the auditors that you know your music (i.e., it's another way of giving specific information with very few words).

Table 3.1. Branding for the Stage Name

Actor	Potential Problem	Solution
Vanessa Williams	Another actress with the same name	Vanessa L. Williams
Leroy Walton	Another actor with the same name	LeRoy Walton
Jessica Michelle Martin	Too stuffy; not "fun" enough	Jess Martin
Eric Joseph Gomez	Marketing non-Latino	Eric McKinley
Tiffany Roma	Too generic	Tiff Roma

Next, list your union affiliations (AEA, SAG/AFTRA, American Guild of Musical Artists [AGMA], etc.). If you are an Equity-membership candidate, you should proudly list this as well. However, if you are not in any of the unions, do not list nonunion; simply list nothing. And remember: There is no shame in not being a member of the unions; just about everyone at one time in their career worked as a nonunion actor/performer.

The next challenge in making the resume specific is the contact information. Do not ever include anything other than a mobile number, an e-mail address, and a website. Please remove your address and social security number if you currently have this on yours (I promise I won't tell anybody if you take it off now). Unless you are signing a contract, you should never, ever provide this information.

There was a time when actors would list other specific information, such as hair and eye color; however, with black-and-white headshots going the way of the dinosaur, this is no longer necessary. With that said, you may still include them if your gut tells you to do so. Your sense of style must continue to make its way into your resume.

In addition, although the inclusion of specific height is still standard, listing the actor's weight is now, for some reason, optional. Ladies often list a dress size instead of their weight, but I have been told by a few casting directors that this is just a way of telling the auditor that you may be hiding something. I would recommend that you go ahead and list your height and weight, as this is what you are marketing. It's not as if you would want to hide any of it; this is what you are selling, so be specific and proud of it. As long as it all matches and comes together to create a marketable type, you will do well to list all of it. Again, trust your gut—it is *your* resume and has to match your personality and sense of style.

The next major category is experience or roles played. Standard formatting for this is three columns. Our eyes are used to this, so please do not stray from this. The three columns include the following three sections: roles, shows, and location/producing company/director.

In the third column, consider listing a production company and director only if you believe that they will help you to gain the auditor's trust. These names should be well-known entities; listing on your resume a college friend who directed you will only serve to cloud the resume. I recommend that you list only recognizable names that will elevate the level of your work. Auditors need to *trust* you, and part of this trust comes from knowing that you have worked with people whom they know and can contact for a reference. This happens a lot, so be strategic in this.

In the roles category, be sure to notate if you have been an understudy, a swing, a standby, or a dance captain. This type of specificity is essential, especially for the younger actor. If you are more of a television or film actor, then list if you have played a lead, supporting role, or featured role instead of the name of the role. Directors and producers are more apt to hire a very talented yet unknown actor as an understudy than in the actual role. This is a great way of building trust. In fact, many young musical theatre performers have debuted on Broadway as a swing—it's a rite of passage for many.

The only time you should not list a specific role is under your commercial category. Regardless of the number of impressive commercials that you have shot, the standard listing for this category is "Conflicts available upon request." This tells the auditor that you have worked in commercials without overdoing it. If they want to know specifics, they will ask you.

Now, under your training and education category, you must list well-known teachers, reputable training studios, and, of course, degrees earned. This area is often the most important category for younger actors or those with relatively fewer credits. Also, this is not the place to be general, as auditors will often not hire someone unless they recognize a name or two on his or her resume. Therefore, be as specific as possible. Do not list the classes that you have taken unless these are specialty classes resulting in some sort of certification or special skill (e.g., stage combat, clowning).

Finally, the last, and often most important, category of the resume is special skills. The standard order for this category is the following: languages spoken, dialects mastered, instruments played, marketable sports, other areas of expertise, and something that showcases your personality. Please do not list "basic piano" or anything that you do at a basic level. Auditors are not looking for people who are basic at anything. As professional agent Jed Abrahams with KMR and Associates has advised up-and-coming talent, this is an industry of experts, so list only those skills that you can perform with great proficiency.

Dialects are marketable skills, and languages are important for larger markets that cast multiethnic talent. Instruments are trendy as well; there was a wave of Broadway musicals between 1998 and 2006 that utilized a company of actors, each of whom also doubled as the musicians in the orchestra (revivals of *Cabaret*, *Sweeney Todd*, and *Company*). Again, only list the instruments if you play them well.

As previously mentioned, this is also the area where you can allow the personality portion of your USPs to shine. If you are a determined type of person, driven, and a risk-taker, your ability to play endurance sports like track and field and water polo may be an asset. If you are warm, grounded, and nurturing, listing "works well with children and animals" would be extremely beneficial in telling the auditors what you are like outside of the rehearsal studio (e.g., what you will be like during breaks or in the dressing room).

Last, actors often list something funny or quirky at the end of their special skills category. This is acceptable as long as funny or quirky is what you are marketing. This is one way you can maximize your USPs without even saying a word. Oftentimes, this section becomes a conversation starter, so be prepared to discuss or perform impressions if this is a special skill listed on your resume. Remember: Your resume will tell the auditors where you might fit in their production; if you follow this with an audition monologue or song that reinforces your USPs, then you will likely earn the callback.

And this, my friend, is how specificity in your resume works!

MK Johnson

mk-johnson.com
555.222.1234
mkjohnson2012@gmail.com

Height: 5'8"   Hair: Light Brown   Eyes: Green   Vocal Type: Soprano/Belt, D3-G5

Theatre

42nd Street Eileen Grace, Chor.	Gladys (Anytime Annie U/S)	Mill Mountain Playhouse, VA
Pippin Matthew Glover, Chor.	Featured Dancer	Highlands Playhouse, NC
9 to 5	Featured Dancer	Highlands Playhouse, NC
Sweet Charity Julio Agustin, Chor.	Nickie *Irene Ryan Nomination*	Forbes Center for the Performing Arts
The Wild Party (Lippa) Julio Agustin, Chor.	Swing/Dance Captain	Forbes Center
The Cherry Orchard Ben Lambert, Dir.	Liubóv Ranyévskaya	Forbes Center
Clybourne Park	Betsy/Lindsay *Irene Ryan Nomination*	Forbes Center
Boeing Boeing	Gretchen	Forbes Center

Education & Training

James Madison University, BA in Musical Theatre
Broadway Dance Center Training Program (Bonnie Erickson, Director)
Broadway Theatre Project Apprentice (Darren Gibson, Artistic Director)

Voice   David Sabella-Mills, Mana Allen, Kate Arecchi, Brenda K. Witmer, Jeremy Mossman, Marina Gillman, Roger Beale, Chris Hall

Acting   Erik Liberman, Ann Morrison, Ben Lambert, Wolf J. Sherrill, Ingrid DeSanctis, Terry Dean, Kate Arecchi, Chris Hall

Dance   Julio Agustin, J.T. Hornstein, Ricky Tripp, Darren Gibson, Debra McWaters, Herman Payne, Garfield Lemonius, Cynthia Thompson

Special Skills

Acoustic rhythm guitar, pop/contemporary music arrangements, basic piano, dance captain, choreography, basic ASL, throws a perfect spiral, can operate skid steers & shoot a gun, Reba McIntyre impression
Dialects: Upper German, North-Central American dialects, Southern American dialects
GA driver's license, Valid US Passport

Sample of a specific resume. *Courtesy of MK Johnson.*

Jared Starkey

(860)-428-7891
Jaredstarkey16@gmail.com
www.JaredStarkey.com
Tenor

Height: 5'7"   Weight: 140lbs

REGIONAL THEATRE

A Chorus Line	Mark	Playhouse on Park
Sweeney Todd	Tobias	Woodstock Playhouse
Chitty Chitty Bang Bang	Goran	Dir./Chor. Merete Muenter
Spring Awakening	Reinhold/Ernst (u/s)	Woodstock Playhouse
Oklahoma!	Jess/Ensemble	Woodstock Playhouse
The Events (Int. Festival of Arts and Ideas)	Choir Member	Yale Repertory Theater

THEATRE

*Parade***	Frankie Epps	Dir. Tim Howard
*Anne of Green Gables**	Gilbert Blythe	Dir. John Hickok
Little Women (Feat. Jan Neuberger)	Laurie	Dir. Julio Agustin
The Green Bird	Renzo	Dir. Sal Trapani

Upcoming*
Kennedy Center American College Theatre Festival 2016 Award for "Outstanding Musical"**

TRAINING

Western Connecticut State University:	*Bachelor of Arts in Musical Theatre* (In Progress)
Acting:	Julio Agustin, Tim Howard, Pam McDaniel, Sal Trapani
Voice:	Deborah Lifton, Janelle Robinson, Howard Kilik
Dance:	Elizabeth Parkinson (Ballet, Jazz), Julio Agustin (Ballet, Musical Theatre Jazz), Scott Wise (Acro)
Master Classes:	Kevin Gray, Jen Rudin, Gabrielle Berberich, Brett Goldstein, Derrick Evans

SPECIAL SKILLS

Dialects:	Australian, Southern (Georgian, Texan)
Movement:	Russians, Front Handspring, Cartwheel, One Handed Cartwheel, Handstands, Hand Walking, Dive Roll, Somersaults, Lifts, Switch Leaps
Sports:	Soccer, Volleyball, Hiking, Skiing, Swimming, Basketball, Biking
Other:	High Falsetto, Whistles, Licensed Driver

Sample of a specific resume. *Courtesy of Jared Starkey.*

Resume Strategy 2: Be Concise

It is often a desire for actors to want to list a ton of stuff, including every credit that they have ever earned. Yet on the working actor's resume, more is not necessarily more. Actors love to list each and every one of their credits in an effort to demonstrate that they have worked. This is not necessarily a good thing. Once your resume has reached the point where it is beginning to look overly crowded, you need to delete a credit each time that you add one. Considering that the resume is no more than one 8×10-inch page, this becomes essential. Make a game of it; this can also motivate you to continue working your way up the ladder of the industry. Think of this: Add a regional theatre credit, delete a college credit; add a national tour credit, delete a theme park credit; add a Broadway credit, delete a regional theatre credit. Now is it sounding like fun?

Another way of making your resume as concise as possible is to omit those credits that you have outgrown; these will only serve to confuse the casting director. I know of a child actress who is now in her early twenties who lists one Broadway credit from her younger years as a way of demonstrating that she has been in the business for a very long time. However, she has removed all other credits from this age range, as she is no longer marketing that person. Can you see how, if she had decided to list more than the one credit, this would be confusing to current auditors?

Finally, also important in making the resume concise is to *choose the smallest number of words to give the most information.* "Dance—ballet/jazz/tap" is stronger and has more weight than "Dance—10 years of ballet, 7 years of jazz, and 3 years of tap." Yes, the latter is much more specific, but it is overkill.

Another example of less-is-more is found in the words chosen. For example, "BFA in Theatre with a minor in Business Adminis-tration" is less strong and not as concise as "BFA in Theatre/Minor in Business Administration." The second example has very subtle differences, but again, it is essential to keeping the information on the resume as tight and concise as possible.

NATHALY LOPEZ
AEA

OFF-BROADWAY

What's It All About?	Performer/Dance Captain	NYTW
Bacharach Reimagined		Dir: Steven Hoggett

NATIONAL/INTERNATIONAL TOUR

Kooza	Soul Singer	Cirque du Soleil
		Dir: Ron Kellum
In the Heights (2nd National)	u/s Daniela & Carla, ensemble, Bolero Singer, radio voice	Worklight Productions Assoc. Dir: Michael Balderrama

THEATRE

Alice by Heart	Queen of Hearts	Theatre Aspen
		Dir: Lear deBessonet
The Groove Factory	Fuschia Flowers/Dance Captain	NYMF 2012
		Dir: Tom Wojtunik
Crazy Head Space	Eating Disorder/PMS	Choice Theatricals
		Dir: Gabriel Barre
Ain't Misbehavin'	Nell	Harlem Repertory Theatre
		Dir: Keith Lee Grant
It Ain't Nothin' But the Blues	Performer	New Haarlem Arts Theatre
		Dir: Alfred Preisser

FILM

Hypebeasts (Short)	Supporting	Dir: Jess Dela Merced

TRAINING

BA in Theater: The City College of New York
Film/TV Acting: Rogues West- Vancouver, BC/ T. Schreiber Studios- NYC/ The Barrow Group- NYC

Singing	Liz Caplan, Julio Agustin
Commercial Acting	T. Schreiber Studios
Movement	Steven Hoggett, Keith Lee Grant
Musical Directors	Alex Lacamoire, David John Madore

SPECIAL SKILLS
+ alto w/ Belt (C5)
+ fluent in spanish
+ recording artist: Nat Lopez (iTunes, Amazon, Google Play, Spotify, etc.)
+ rapping, excellent harmony skills, whistling, ghetto talk, character voices
+ cooking, jogging
+ basic dance styles: hip pop, salsa, merengue, bachata, jazz, musical theatre

www.natlopez.com
nat@natlopez.com

Sample of a concise resume. *Courtesy of Nathaly Lopez.*

Resume Strategy 3: Be Clear

Last but not least, the amount of space you include in a resume is almost as important as the amount of information given. It doesn't help you if you have so much on your resume that it becomes difficult to locate the most important roles. Find ways to insert space into your resume by deleting nonessential credits.

First of all, insert space between the headings (e.g., "Theatre," "TV/Film," "Commercials," "Training," and "Special Skills"). Make certain that each category is easy to find, and *please* be sure that the columns in each line up. There is nothing worse than a muddled, confusing, overcooked resume; this is a sign of someone who is not secure and doesn't know what he or she is marketing.

The working actor's resume must be easy to read. Do not make the casting director strain her eyes or work too hard to find something—because she won't! The most important quality of a working resume is that it is clear and indicative of *who* you are, *what* your particular strengths are, and *how* you should be cast. You will do this by listing similar roles together and keeping categories separate. If you are a musical theatre performer, then list these credits first, followed by classical theatre (as they are both heightened theatre), then contemporary works. If you are a dancer first with dance-captain experience, then highlight this by first listing roles in which you've been dance captain or lead dancer, followed by other strong movement work. So you see, keeping things together allows auditors to focus on the area that is most impressive to them. Otherwise, they have to jump back and forth from one credit to another—something that's impossible to do in the two to three seconds that they have!

A few final notes: Remember that everyone starts their career with nothing, so avoid the desire to lie or even exaggerate your credits. Do not stress if you are a beginning actor or transitioning (from chorus to roles, stage to film, etc.). Show business is a small, small, small world, and you will inevitably be caught if you stretch the truth. If you do not have that many credits, then showcase your training or highlight your special skills or focus on stating names of people with whom you have worked or studied.

Also, resumes must be updated very, very often, so trust that you will constantly be adding credits and other marketable traits and information as you move forward in this industry. Avoid copying your resume directly on your headshot, as you will inevitably have to update this in the next six months, and you do not want to have to throw away a stack of headshots.

ARIEL PACHECO
SAG-AFTRA Eligible
646-353-5865
ariel@arielpacheco.com

Height 5'11   **Eyes** Dark Brown
Hair Black   **Weight** 160 lbs.

FILM

EXPOSED	Supporting	LIONSGATE/Starring KEANU REEVES
AN INAPPROPRIATE AFFECT	Lead	Dir. Russ Martin
SPLIT DECISION*	Supporting	Dirs. Antoine Allen and Edmar Flores

*WINNER - Action on Film Award for Best LGBT Project,
*WINNER - Urban Media Makers Film Festival 2013 Founder's Award

TV/WEB

MY CRAZY LOVE	Guest-Star	Oxygen
CELEBRITY CRIME FILES 'LYMON BOSTOCK"	Co-Star	TV One Network
IF YOUR WINGMAN HAD AN AIR FORCE	Featured	College Humor
SECOND-HAND NY	Series Regular	Second-Hand NY Productions
**Miami Web Fest Official Selection		
HOW TO BE A BRIT IN AMERICA	Guest-Star	How to be a Brit In America Prods.

THEATRE

WHEN THE CLOUDS COVER THE SUN	Joseph/Lead	BAM Media Group, NY
		Dir. Brandon Wright
RIFF RAFF	Mike Leon/Lead	City College, NY
DE DONDE	Pedro/Lead	City College, NY
DOG SEES GOD	Matt/Lead	City College, NY
DAY OF ABSENCE	Mayor H. E. Lee/Lead	City College, NY
TURNING POINTS	Timothy/Lead	City College, NY

INDUSTRIALS
List Upon Request

TRAINING
Graduated/Certificate from the New York Conservatory of Dramatic Arts***
***Selected as part of a "Super Jury" of twenty actors from the graduating class.

ACTING	Jay R. Goldenberg, John Tyrell, Becky London, Maury Ginsburg, Ela Thier, Julio Matos, Carol Kastendiek, Meghan Duffy, Eugene Nesmith David Willinger, Steve Pulmetter, Rawleigh Moreland, Tom O'Brien, Cobey Mandarino
COMMERCIALS	David Cady, Richard Larson, Lane Binkley
IMPROV	Judith Searcy

SKILLS
FLUENT IN SPANISH. Great at Latte Art! Jet Skied in Malibu! Quad Biked around Aruba! Dialects include British, Cockney, Standard British, Middle Eastern, Spanish, Russian. Impersonations, Rapper, Very Good Basketball Player, Good Football Player, Weight Lifting, Licensed Driver (NY), Valid U.S. Passport.

Sample of a clear resume. *Courtesy of Ariel Pacheco.*

And finally, depending on your experience, consider creating a separate resume for the various genres of acting (e.g., theatre, musical theatre, television, and film). You are probably marketing something different in each genre and must be certain that you define clear USPs for each. Credits in each are listed in a different order and market a relatively different person. Most young actors prefer to create one sole resume until they have achieved enough credits in other areas to merit the organization and management of keeping separate resumes. Trust that you will know when it's time to create a separate resume for each of the various genres of work.

And remember that, on a resume, more is not more. When it comes to a theatrical resume, being *specific*, *concise*, and *clear* is the way to go.

Success Strategy 4

———————○———————

Take That
"Perfect" Headshot

THERE ARE COUNTLESS BOOKS written on the subject of professional headshots, including what makes a good headshot, how to choose the right photographer, ways to prepare for the photo shoot, and strategies for selecting the perfect shot. In my opinion, the market is already inundated with books offering suggestions on this topic; because of this, I had considered omitting this chapter entirely for fear of adding to the already-crowded market. Instead, I have opted to provide you with a streamlined approach, while also focusing on how to maximize the headshot as a viable tool for promoting your career as a working professional.

True or False: Taking the "perfect" headshot can make the difference between having a career in today's industry and not having a career.
Answer: True. In today's industry, where so much casting is done by online submissions and so much work is based on a look or a clearly defined type, having the perfect headshot can make the difference between working and not working. It is just that important.

By and large, our industry as a whole employs typecasting as one of its core foundations. Judging a book by its cover is perfectly acceptable, even expected, in the performing arts. Of course, your

34

headshot will not get you the job, but *not* having a strong, compelling, and clearly marketable headshot can, and will, often prevent you from even being considered for an initial audition.

Consider the following examples of before and after headshots that include each actor's unique selling points. Imagine how much easier each actor has made the job of the casting director with the headshot that more clearly markets their brand!

Actor 1: Jared Starkey

USPs: energetic and determined, boyishly charming, awkwardly quirky

Courtesy of Jared Starkey; photos by Joe Loper.

Actor 2: Awilda Cantres

USPs: ambitious, exotic romantic, free-spirited

Courtesy of Awilda Cantres; photos by Brian Offidani.

At the end of this chapter is an essential homework assignment that you need to complete prior to moving forward with your photo shoot. The homework is a chance for you to combine your USPs with the following six strategies for preparing, selecting, and reproducing your perfect headshot.

STRATEGIES FOR GETTING THAT "PERFECT" HEADSHOT

Taking the perfect headshot is a multistep process that includes visualizing your ultimate photo, researching photographers, practicing your poses, moving through the actual photo shoot, selecting the top headshot contenders, and reproducing your selected shots. Many casting directors refer to the headshot as the stage actor's calling card. It is still the most important aspect of getting seen for an audition for stage and commercial work—more important than a resume full of credits or a website full of videos. In two seconds or less of glancing at your headshot, the casting professional will make a determination as to whether you are worth considering for a project, as well as where exactly you might fit into that project. Because of this urgency, it is of the utmost importance that you spend as much time, effort, and, yes, money as necessary in order to help you get the most perfect headshot possible, one that will give you the greatest chance of sustaining a career as a working professional.

Six Steps to the Perfect Headshot

1. Visualize.
2. Research and interview professional photographers.
3. Prepare for the shoot.
4. Take the photo.
5. Select the perfect headshot.
6. Reproduce.

Headshot Strategy 1: Visualize

This section contains a worksheet for you to use in the beginning phases of your headshot process. The purpose of this homework is to get you to visualize what your headshot will look like even before you have taken the photos. You have to consider what angles work for you, whether to do a simple headshot or a half-body or three-quarter shot, what colors to wear, what textures to consider, what environment is most suitable, and what expressions to market. A lot of this is ultimately up to your headshot photographer, but it is part of your job to provide her with as much information as possible about yourself and what you are seeking. It helps if you can take a moment right now to review your USPs so that we know exactly what we are looking to get into the photo. Please take a moment to rewrite your USPs here:

_____

_____

_____

This exercise can be a lot of fun if you allow yourself to enjoy it. Part of the process entails creating a collage of other actors' headshots that inspire you. By exploring what others in your type or category are wearing, doing, and marketing, you can become clearer as to what works and what does not work. It will help you to select the clothing that is appropriate for the shot, including eliminating options that you love but will confuse people regarding your established brand. It will also work in your favor as you begin to create a clear working relationship with those in the industry who are seeking someone *like* you. Although everyone is unique, nobody is an original. The "perfect" headshot supports this.

There is a saying that 80 percent of the people for whom you audition are not seeking anyone your type. Therefore, the goal is not to impress every single person for whom you audition but to make a strong impression on the 20 percent of those people who are! Therefore, if your photo is not clear and is so generic and trying to impress everyone, it will impress no one. You will wind up missing out on projects for which you are qualified because of a lack of clarity in the photo.

Headshot Strategy 2: Research and Interview Professional Photographers

Part 2 of the process is to interview and ultimately select the perfect headshot photographer for you. Those who are early-career professionals may simply wish to research a headshot photographer's work based on recommendations from your coach, mentor, or peers. If you have an agent, be sure to seek out recommendations from him or her, as many agents prefer that their clients shoot with photographers from their rosters. If you have industry contacts, use them as a resource as well.

I also highly recommend that you interview at least three headshot photographers to make certain not only that you feel comfortable with them but also that they also *get* you. Just like finding a voice teacher or acting coach, selecting the right headshot photographer is a very personal experience—not everyone is the right fit. Just because someone else raved about a certain photographer does not mean that you will have the same positive connection to them. Also, please do your homework, and if possible, interview them *in person*.

You must also make certain that the headshot photographer is a *headshot* photographer. There are certain photographers who pride themselves on being able to photograph weddings, nature, babies, *and* actors; I highly recommend staying away from these unless they are known in the acting industry for their work with actors. Photographing an actor for a headshot is a very specific talent that takes a long time to develop and perfect. Many headshot photographers begin their careers by offering discounted or even free headshots as a way of developing their craft. Do not be afraid to experiment with them, but understand the difference between an apprentice photographer and an established and reputable headshot photographer. Also, the headshot photographer offers very different skills from someone who takes pictures of actors for publicity, commercial print, modeling, or other purposes. You are looking for someone who bills themselves as a *headshot photographer* and nothing more.

When previewing the headshot photographer's portfolio of work, notice the following: Are the eyes the most engaging part of the headshot? Is there energy in the pose, with the actor seeming to have a conversation with the camera? Is the actor marketing a very clear and specific type, essence, and energy? Do the clothing selections support the actor's USPs, or do they seem to contradict themselves? Is the lighting even on both sides, and is shadow used for dramatic effect rather than a lack of lighting skills? Is the background distracting, or does it support the actor's USPs? Is it clearly an actor headshot versus a model or glamour shot?

Researching the Headshot Photographer's Portfolio

1. Eyes
2. Energy
3. Clear USPs
4. Smooth and even lighting
5. Nondistracting background
6. A "perfect" headshot (*not* a model or glamour shot)

Many headshot photographers have a signature style for which they are known; some prefer simple, clean backgrounds, while others prefer environments that support the actor's brand. Joe Loper, creator of Guerrilla Photography in New York City, believes that actors *must* be photographed with honest expressions that come from spontaneous reactions. He wants the industry to "move away from the over-edited, glamorized, and ridiculous posing that's become so popular with headshot photographers. Actors are real people and their headshots should emphasize that."

Basically, as long as the headshot photographer's work is clear, compelling, and draws your focus to the actor's eyes, type, and essence, then you are as good as gold. Remember to trust your gut; some excellent photographers may just not be right for you. While most of my clients trust my recommendations, some prefer to work with other photographers for various reasons (i.e., they just "like" them better). That is more than okay; it is necessary.

Once you find three headshot photographers whose work you value, be sure to interview them. Ask them questions about cost, number of photos taken, and retouched photos provided; details regarding the day of the shoot (location, time, music, pets—yes, pets); and speed of receipt of proofs. It is best to visit the headshot photographers' studios in person to make certain they do not have pets (for those of you with allergies) and that they are in a safe and comfortable location for you. If you are uncomfortable, then it will show in the shots.

Last, in today's market, you should be able to find a strong headshot photographer whose work is both affordable and of a high caliber. Be careful of paying for boutique headshots just to work with a high-end photographer unless, of course, there is something unique about her work (and you have boutique funds). The best headshots highlight *you*, not the photographer. If a director asks you who took your shots, then you probably used the wrong photographer.

The following is a sample of a clear, compelling, clearly branded headshot.

Actor 3: Eric McKinley

USPs: takes direction, endearing, larger than life, easygoing

Courtesy of Eric Gomez; photos by Joe Loper.

Headshot Strategy 3: Prepare for the Shoot

In preparing for your photo shoot, be sure to drink lots of water, get plenty of rest, and stay away from the sun. Also, ask your headshot photographer if he or she would like a copy of your headshot homework in advance to know what you are seeking out of this shoot. Most will not be offended and will see you as an informed actor, while some may prefer that you use it for your own preparation. Both are acceptable; the homework is really to help you to feel as prepared as possible.

**Headshot Strategies 4 and 5: Take the Photo
and Select the Perfect Headshot**

Now that you have taken a bunch of fabulous headshots, it is time
to begin the search for the "perfect" one. Even if you are less than
thrilled about the shoot (it happens to all of us at one time or another), do not be discouraged; remember that all you need is one
great shot, and there is usually one great shot in even the worst
photo shoot.

In beginning to click through each headshot photo, I suggest
compiling a group of about thirty to sixty of your favorite shots (depending on the number of shots taken). The most important thing
is that you *select only those photos that look like you on a good day.*
Younger actors love to choose the ones that make them look like
models (I call them "glamour shots"). Unless you are marketing
"model" as one of your USPs, do not choose a photo that is too beautiful. Casting directors become furious when the headshot in front
of them does not look like the person who stands before them. The
headshot should look like the actor at his best and nothing more.

And, by the way, if you have altered your looks in any way
since the photo shoot (e.g., dyed your hair, shaved your beard,
gained fifteen pounds), then it's time to schedule a new headshot
session. I repeat: The headshot must look like you on a good day,
and that good day is *today!* This is a business; therefore, make sure
that the photo represents a clear type (i.e., clearly indicates how
to cast you).

The way I assist clients in selecting headshots is to separate the
top thirty or so into the following categories: theatrical (for stage
work), television and film (these can be separated for those with
sufficient credits in both categories), commercial, and commercial
print (for those exploring that venue).

With your USPs in mind, begin to compare each shot, two by
two, each time deleting the weaker of the two shots. When you are
comparing two very strong and comparable shots, you might want to
print them on regular paper to compare the nuances in each. Look
for very minor but recognizable differences in the eyes (openness),
the smile (relaxed), the wisps of hair, and the energy that is emitted
from the shot (angles).

Because the eyes are the most important feature, be sure that they are alive and interacting with the lens (your scene partner). It should seem as if you were photographed in the middle of a scene and not posing for a picture. A model poses; an actor acts. Select the shot that is most active.

Eventually you will have compared the photos two by two until you are left with your top pick in each category. In the beginning, you may decide to limit the number of headshots that you reproduce so that you do not confuse people in the industry. The more you can use the same shot (or two shots), the more people will become familiar with your brand and begin to trust you. Remember this when creating your website as well; more shots are not always better. Young actors get excited and want to reproduce their many looks. However, one strong, simple, and clear headshot is the best option.

Headshot Strategy 6: Reproduce

The headshot has been planned, prepared, taken, and finally selected. Now it is time to reproduce the shot and prepare it for distribution.

In selecting a reproduction company, I suggest that you ask actors in your area for the most affordable professional headshot reproduction company. Find a company that provides a quality product for bulk copies, is affordable, and can quickly reproduce if necessary. This is not something that you should spend a lot of money on; trust that you will have plenty of things to spend your money on in your quest for work.

You want to reproduce your headshots in bulk, perhaps fifty to two hundred of each shot, depending on the market in your area and your tenacity in attending open calls. The headshots must have your name on the actual shot; whether you have a border is completely up to your individual taste. The reproductions do not have to be expensive, but they do need to be of a professional quality. Many established reproduction companies will accept a digital file from your photographer so that you do not have to handle any aspect of the process (except paying for them, of course). They can even mail them to you if you are out of state.

If you are picking the headshots up from the company, request to see a proof prior to the reproductions to make certain that they are to your satisfaction. Once they have been printed in bulk, the company will not redo them for you unless they admit to having made the error (and this is almost always impossible to prove).

Now that you have picked up your headshots, you must begin to attach your resume copies to the backs. Make certain that you have cut your resumes to the standard 8 × 10-inch size. Staple your resumes to the headshots, one staple on each of the four corners. Do not photocopy your resume onto your headshot; you are a working professional and will be updating your resume quite frequently. If you cannot detach your outdated resume from your headshot, then you will have just wasted your photos.

My suggestion is that you always have a file or drawer full of about twelve to twenty resumes and headshots already stapled and ready to go. This is an industry in which being prepared counts; the goal is to be so busy that you don't even have time to staple your resume to your headshot when preparing for an audition. You want this to be the case for yourself, so prepare for this.

MAXIMIZE YOUR HEADSHOT USAGE

As suggested earlier, update your website with your new headshot. In addition, you must also complete your marketing package with the following tools: resume, business cards, postcards, and e-mail signature.

Always have about twelve to twenty headshots already stapled to your resume. Do not wait until you go to an audition to staple your shots, as anything that can go wrong will go wrong (you may lose or break your stapler or run out of time at the audition) and you will be seen as an underprepared actor.

Create or update your business cards with one look (or two, as long as both support *one* clear set of USPs). Be certain that your business card contains your name, telephone number, e-mail address, and website. Make sure that the photo is large enough to make an impact. Be careful of putting too much on the card.

Print postcards that contain your headshot for keeping your network updated; we cover this in chapter 14. This is an essential marketing tool and, like the business cards, can be purchased in bulk for very little money.

Finally, add your headshot to your e-mail signature, and make certain that this goes out automatically with each and every correspondence. The e-mail signature might include your USPs spelled out, a favorite quote, a one-sentence promotional of your goings-on, a link to your website, and your headshot at the bottom. People have to get used to seeing your headshot in order to begin to trust you, so sending it out with every e-mail is an easy way to do this. Also, do not expect that they will take the time to click on your attachments; give it to them in the e-mail to ensure that they will see it.

The following are clear examples of a strong signature.

Danyel Fulton

Actress/Singer

(212) 555-1212

www.danyelfulton.com

Recently seen as "Dani" in the opening number

for the first annual BroadwayCon!

Courtesy of Danyel Fulton.

Erin McNerney

Actress/Dancer/Singer

ErinMcNerney.com

212-555-1313

abc@dmail.com

Dedicated. Consistent. Fun.

Courtesy of Erin McNerney.

TOP HEADSHOT MISTAKES MADE BY ACTORS

A Glamour Shot Is Not a Headshot

I know, I know—it is so exciting to get new headshots; the possibilities are endless now that you have brand-new professional headshots. You can almost feel your career taking off—you never even knew that you were this gorgeous!

Whoa! This is not the time to start changing your USPs. Please do not choose the prettiest shot taken of you, unless pretty is one of the qualities that you are marketing. If you tend to play roles that are glamorous, then you can definitely select a shot that highlights this quality. If, instead, your roles tend to be quirky or sassy, more of a character actor's essence, then go for more of a character shot—less traditionally pretty, more fun and out of the box.

Everyone wants to be beautiful and sexy; however, sexy is not a matter of looks, but of confidence. If you push the pretty, then you will likely type yourself into an entirely different category, confuse the auditors, and make it harder to get work. Remember: Casting directors want a headshot that looks like *you* on a good day—and *you* is defined by your USPs. Anything outside of this is pure waste.

Do Not Scrimp on the Headshot

I have coached clients at various levels in their careers. It does not matter whether they are college age or established in their forties; actors are almost always on a strict budget. This is the reason I recommend exploring at least three headshot photographers at a time in order to comparison shop.

The good news for actors is that, at the time of this printing, due to the climbing number of strong photographers, most legitimate headshot photographers have reduced their prices. You can get a great, quality headshot at an affordable rate. So save your pennies and pay for a shot of which you will be proud. A median cost for a strong headshot is between three hundred and six hundred dollars (depending on number and inclusion of hair and makeup). I know actors who have paid one thousand dollars for their headshots, and some who have paid three hundred dollars for their shots, and I was not able to tell the difference between the two. Of course, if the actor felt the need to spend one thousand dollars, then I was not going to discount their feelings. I simply want actors to do their research so that they can find the best option for themselves.

I once paid eight hundred dollars (which was a lot back in the '90s) for shots because I had been working steadily on a production contract and wanted to treat myself to the best photographer possible. The photographer owned a large portfolio of headshots of famous people. In this book, he had the "before" shots from previous photographers and the "after" shots that he had taken. With so much proof, how could I go wrong?

I believe I am the only actor not included in his bible of head-shots. My "after" shots were tragic! This experience did nothing for my wallet or my self-esteem!

Moral of the story: Expensive does not equal better.

That said, "cheap" is not always the way to go, either. You need to save your funds so that you can afford a shot that you are proud to use for one, two, or even five years. Just as your talent and train-ing are the most important part of your audition, the headshot is the most important aspect of your business. Do not scrimp on this!

Please Leave Cousin Ed Out of It

Just because your cousin has a state-of-the-art camera does not make him a headshot photographer any more than my having a stethoscope makes me a doctor! There is an art, as well as a sci-ence, to taking a strong and competitive headshot; this includes an understanding of acting, lighting, art, environment, texture, energy, character, symmetry, and body language. This is difficult to under-stand unless you are, of course, a headshot photographer.

And those, my friends, are suggestions to help you to get that "per-fect" headshot. Please do not hesitate to peruse an article or two or skim through a book or two in order to supplement our discussion. We work in an ever-changing industry, where trends appear and dis-appear very quickly. Be sure that you do not succumb to the latest trends, yet remain open to subtle changes in the headshot industry.

Now say, "Cheese!" and have fun getting ready for your close-up!

THE "PERFECT" HEADSHOT HOMEWORK

I highly suggest that you create a collage by copying and pasting onto a document as many professional actor headshots as possible that coincide with your answers to the questions in the box. This is your headshot collage; refer to this when considering the colors, textures, environments, poses, and cropping that make sense for your type and marketability.

> ### Headshot Homework Questions
>
> Answer the following five questions in as much detail as possible:
>
> 1. What type of roles are you going out for? (List specific roles in theatre, television, film, etc., for which you can clearly be cast.)
> 2. If there was a casting breakdown describing the perfect character for you to play, what would the adjectives for this role be? Begin with "Seeking . . ."
> 3. Are there professional actors currently playing the types of roles you are perfectly suited to play? Make a list of these.
> 4. How would your friends and family describe your personality?
> 5. Is there a specific look you want to go for in your headshot? What do you want it to say?

This homework helps you to become clearer as to what it is that you are trying to capture in your headshot. You may choose to forward it to potential headshot photographers in order to help you to select a photographer that "gets" you, as well as to assist the photographer in being clear as to what it is that you are seeking to capture in the photo shoot.

Sample Headshot Homework

Actor 4: Erin Poland

USPs: reliable, girl next door (with more than meets the eye), whimsical

Courtesy of Erin Poland; photo by Taylor Hooper.

1. What type of roles are you going out for?

   Belle in Beauty and the Beast, *Frenchy in* Grease, *Natalie in* Next to Normal, *Cherry in* Bus Stop, *Holly in* Breakfast at Tiffany's, *Roxie in* Chicago, *Catherine in* Suddenly Last Summer, *Beth in* A Lie of the Mind

2. If there was a breakdown describing the perfect character for you to play, what would the adjectives for this role be?

   Whimsical, cute/sexy, reliable, imaginative

3. Is there a working actor who is having your career, playing the types of roles you should play?

   Anne Hathaway, Zooey Deschanel, Rachel McAdams, Kirsten Dunst, Mila Kunis, a young Audrey Hepburn

4. How would your friends and family describe your personality?

   Determined, bubbly, energetic, animated, warm

5. Is there a specific look you want to go for in your headshot? What do you want it to say?

   Seeking cute/sexy, confident, inviting, more-than-meets-the-eye actress.

Success Strategy 5

Write a Standout Cover Letter

As WE EXAMINE the business of theatre and our quest to become working professionals, it is essential for us to use our creative writing skills to compose a standout cover letter that we can add to our arsenal of the tools of the trade. To be honest, this is not something that most performers consider to be crucial. However, I have discovered that many industry professionals appreciate receiving an introductory note attached to the headshot and resume; it helps them to do their job with greater speed and ease. A brief, descriptive note that informs them of who you are, what you are submitting for, and why they should consider you will give you a leg up over those headshots and resumes that arrive without anything attached. As with every other strategy in this book, developing a standout cover letter gives you an edge and guarantees that you are doing everything within your power to cement your position as a working professional in the industry.

The standout cover letter entices the auditors to consider you for their production in several ways. First and foremost, a brief yet descriptive cover letter helps the casting professional to quickly decide what to do with your materials. Consider that the average casting notice can solicit a response of more than two hundred submissions. Think about it from the casting director's perspective: You have one position to fill and about two hundred to three hundred job applicants. The pressure is on. The casting professional cannot possibly consider every single submission equally; this is where the standout cover letter comes in.

By developing a brief and compelling four-sentence cover letter, you have given yourself the greatest probability that your materials will be considered. I have always contended that there is a science to casting, which is this: Your cover letter receives approximately four seconds of a casting director's time. If a connection was made within those four seconds (and we will discuss how to make that connection), then the casting professional will take one additional second to glance at your headshot and, if still interested, quickly turn it over to peruse your resume for another two to three seconds. And voilà! You have won at the game of self-submissions. By submitting a standout cover letter with your headshot and resume, you have done everything within your power (i.e., your job) to solidify your reputation as a working professional.

Without submitting the cover letter, you are essentially giving the casting director a blind photo without any information; the casting director has to make his own assumptions as to who you are, how to place you in the production, and why he ought to consider you instead of the other 299 applicants. The cover letter would have done all of this for him, thereby allowing him to simply either agree or disagree with you. Without it, he must expend his energy to figure you out. Honestly, how likely do you suppose it is that he will spend all of that energy on someone he does not know?

I am not saying that you are required to do the casting director's job, but making his job just a tad bit easier by submitting a standout cover letter allows him to do his best work *for you*!

PART I: DRAFTING A STANDOUT COVER LETTER IS PART SCIENCE, PART ART!

There are several great tidbits that will excite you about this part of your process. First of all, writing the standout cover letter is part creative, part business, and all you! It is fun to create something that further supports your endeavor of working professionally by putting down on paper why you are deserving of such a worthy goal.

And perhaps the greatest thing about this project is that, once you have created a standout cover letter that really works, you will never have to do it again! Yes, I said that—this is a once-in-a-lifetime project—a gift that goes on giving. My own standout cover letter has morphed over the years with regard to the specific details, but the general shape and wording have essentially remained the same.

Once you have completed yours, all you need to do is adjust the details for each specific audition, and you are that much closer to the audition. You can now focus on the important things—like the actual audition!

The scientific part of the standout cover letter is in the format; this includes your choice of font, the specific content (e.g., clear contact information, descriptive word choice, detailed references, and proof of reliability), and the length of each section (introduction, body, and conclusion). These are discussed at length later.

Where you can get creative and have fun is in selecting the juiciest words for each aspect that you are describing. Such descriptive phrases as *unpredictable risk-taker, effervescent personality,* and *deliciously awkward comedic timing* are ways of accomplishing this. I always use a thesaurus when assisting my clients with their standout cover letters because, although several words may mean the same thing, we want to look for the juiciest, most compelling word choices that will make the greatest impact on the reader.

You also want to choose a font that gives off the energy that you are marketing. There are dozens of fonts from which to choose; depending on your brand, you may select something fun, professional, bold, sensual, classic, awkward, or one of many others.

Third, depending on what you are specifically marketing, you may also decide to invest in a specific resume paper that markets your brand. For mailed submissions, your choice of paper can vary in color and texture. For online submissions, you may decide to add a subtle design or border that impacts the reader in the desired way. However, please note that many casting directors emphasize that this is a waste of money and may give off the impression of an actor who is trying too hard. My advice to you is to always trust your gut—you won't know if something works until you test it.

In conclusion, each of these three—specificity in wording, selection of font, and resume style—combine to give a strong and clear impression as to who you are and that you are deserving of careful consideration.

PART II: WAYS TO INCLUDE YOUR USPs

As with every marketing tool that you have added to your arsenal, the basic tenet is to consistently reinforce your brand and to not confuse people. This also goes for your standout cover letter, in which you must highlight what you are specifically marketing—that is, your unique selling points. Including your USPs in your standout cover letter is essential because they give the reader subliminal messages about what it would be like to work with you (reputation and work ethic), if you would be right for one of the roles they are casting (type), and what you are like outside of the rehearsal process (personality).

I always recommend that you include your name somewhere at the top of the stationery as a sort of logo. Consider the type of font that you use as a way of hinting at your personality. It is best if you replicate the font used in your resume.

By using a specific and impactful font for your name, you have just converted your signature into an easily recognizable logo that

Samples of Fonts That Reinforce the Actor's USPs

Ima Funnygirl (Comic Sans)
Ima Funnygirl (Ar Essence)
Ima Funnygirl (Curlz)

JACK MCJOCK (GOUDY STOUT)
Jack McJock (Bauhaus)
Jack McJock (Cooper Black)

Tina Theatre-Geek (Broadway)
Tina Theatre-Geek (Playbill)
TINA THEATRE-GEEK (CASTELLAR)

serves to define who you are and what you are marketing to anyone who comes across it.

In addition, the size of the font should be quite a bit larger than that of the rest of the letter. I recommend that you use a traditional font, typically Times New Roman, for the rest of the standout cover letter. Remember that this is a business letter; you will have plenty of opportunities to insert your personality into the content of the letter, so keep the text recognizable and reliable.

Next after your name is your contact information. Here you include your phone number, your e-mail address, and your website. Note: If you are working with an agent, do not include your personal information; only their information is necessary because they are serving as your representative. Also, unlike the standard business cover letter, do not include your return address on this—and never, ever include your social security number!

You should also include the date somewhere in this area, perhaps a space or two below your contact information. Oftentimes, the casting professional does not feel that you are right for this project for which you have submitted, but your materials have made such a strong impact on them that they decide to keep your materials on file for future consideration. Hence, the date of your submission serves to remind them of your previous contact.

One difference between the standard business cover letter and the standout theatrical cover letter is that you may choose to omit the address of the person you are contacting. As discussed, your goal is to include only essential information, and because they probably know their own address, this information becomes extraneous. There is no space on the standout cover letter for anything extraneous, so do not include their address.

We are now in the greeting of the letter. The words *Dear (name of recipient)* are always followed by a colon (unless you have a personal relationship with them, in which case you use a comma). This is a place where many people fall apart and insult the recipient. Always, always, always refer to the casting professional as Mr., Ms., or Mrs., unless you have already established a personal relationship with them. Beginning the greeting with Mr., Ms., or Mrs. shows a level of respect that is essential to your professional dealings. Even

Broadway actors often refer to playwrights, directors, and producers as Mr. and Ms. out of the extreme respect that they have for the work that they do. Therefore, refer to casting professionals by their title and last name only until you have transitioned onto a first-name basis. How do you know when you are on a first-name basis? They will tell you!

Another common mistake artists make is sending a generic letter with no specific recipient. *To Whom It May Concern* is unacceptable, as it indicates a lack of knowledge as to who the key players are, as well as laziness on your part. You must do your research to find out *exactly* who you need to contact so that you begin to nurture the proper industry relationships. You can always telephone the office to confirm if the person you believe is the contact person is, indeed, the person in charge of that project. For example, consider calling and saying something like this: "Hi. This is Julio Agustin, and I just wanted to confirm that Mr. John Smith is still the head of casting for *My Big, Fat Juicy Musical.* . . . Great. Thank you for your assistance." Simple, safe, and sufficient.

In addition to confirming the person's name, *please confirm both the spelling of their name and their gender.* How disrespected do you think the casting professional feels when you don't even bother to get his name right? And imagine how "Ms. Francis Smith" feels when Ms. Francis is a mister or "Mr. Sam Smith" was born a woman and has no plans to transition! If your research has not been helpful in answering these questions, then you have every right to call the office and, similar to the previous example, request to confirm the spelling and gender of the recipient.

On the following page is an example of the greeting for the standout cover letter. Refer to it as you create your own.

PART III: THE WHO AND WHAT, WHY, AND WHEN OF THE STANDOUT COVER LETTER

You are probably already familiar with the three parts of the standard cover letter (i.e., the introduction, the body, and the conclusion). Although we also adhere to this format, our standout cover letter has slight variations to each of the three sections.

TIFF ROPER

(123) 555-7890

tiffroper@abc.net

June 18, 2020

Dear Mr. Smith:

I am an experienced comedic actress with a strong command of the English language and am thrilled to submit for the role of Beatrice in your upcoming *Much Ado about Nothing.*

I have experience playing comedic roles, such as Nurse in a recent production of William Shakespeare's *Romeo and Juliet,* and have worked closely with your choreographer, John Jones, who can attest to my performing skills and overall reliability.

I will be calling you on Thursday to schedule an appointment for the invited call, and thank you in advance for your time and careful consideration.

Sincerely,

Tiff

Tiffany Roper

The Who and What

The first paragraph of the standout cover letter is the introduction. This section briefly answers the questions of "who" and "what" of each particular submission. In stating *who* you are, you need to include something that piques the casting professional's interest. You can begin with your name or a brief description of who you are. Mentioning your full name is important if it matches the role or production for which you are submitting. For example, "My name is Rosa Martinez" for a regional production of *In the Heights* would be an asset because this is a traditionally Latino musical about the culture of Washington Heights in New York City.

I had the pleasure of sharing my Broadway debut alongside Brad Bradley, an incredibly talented character actor, singer, and dancer who has earned a wealth of New York credits, especially in his work on comedic roles. I can only assume that his catchy name supported what he was marketing—fun and quirky—and may have even helped him to cement his reputation in the industry. This is a specific example of how subtle information can be extremely effective in defining your "who."

The second part of the introduction answers the "what" (i.e., *what you are submitting for*), the name of the show for which you wish to be considered and, even better, the role that you are perfectly suited to portray. "I am an experienced comedic actress with a strong command of the English language and am thrilled to submit for the role of Beatrice in your upcoming production of *Much Ado about Nothing*." If you are a comedic character actress with excellent language skills, submitting for the season of summer stock musicals is a long shot; however, submitting for this role of Beatrice, or for the role of Nurse in a production of William Shakespeare's *Romeo and Juliet*, will surely get you noticed!

The introduction of the standout cover letter gives a brief, clear, and specific introduction of *who* you are and *what* you are submitting for—which will inevitably give you an extra second of consideration for the audition. Take a few minutes now to begin working on a standout introduction for your cover letter.

The Why

The body of the standout cover letter encompasses the best parts of your resume and condenses this information into about two sentences. The most important question to answer in the body is this: Why should the creative team invite *you* to audition?

Let us say that, of the three hundred submissions that a casting professional receives for each production, about seventy-five of them are vying for the same part as you are. However, by submitting a standout cover letter that answers why you are the most worthy of consideration, you have done your job to highlight your abilities and gain the casting professional's trust.

Some examples of specific reasons a casting professional might consider you for a role include:

- *You have previously played the role* (this means that you already know the lines and music and need less time to rehearse).
- *You have played similar roles to the one in question* (this means that you have proven experience playing that particular *type*).
- *You have previously worked at the theatre* (again, proven experience).
- *You have previously worked with the director, choreographer, or other creative person on this production* (the trust factor is huge here).
- *You have another tie or connection to this production or the theatre* (this gives them someone to call for a reference).

Again, please refer to your resume, and pick out the strongest details that highlight how your past can be used to benefit their production. The following is an example of the second paragraph (the body) of a submission that was effective in getting this performer seen for an audition. The casting notice read, "Seeking performers for Peppercorn Theatre's summer stock production of *Barnum* (circus skills a plus)":

> From my materials, you will see that I have an eclectic resume of movement skills (e.g., fire-eating, contortion). My experience in such shows as *Pippin* and *The Magic Show* would make me a strong contender for your production. I also recently worked with the production's choreographer on a *Pepsi-Cola* industrial; I am certain that he will attest to my skills and reliability.

From this example, you can see how it would be difficult to bypass this person's headshot and resume given that they answered their "why" with such detail that they appear to be perfect for the production. Use the this example to help you to create your own two- to three-sentence body that answers your *why*. Again, use your resume, and include specific, descriptive words that highlight the qualities that make you uniquely talented and reliable.

The When

The final paragraph of the standout cover letter is called the conclusion. Perhaps a more suitable name is the *call to action*. This final paragraph is a one- to two-sentence clincher that indicates *when you plan to follow up* and also expresses gratitude to the recipient for their time and consideration.

A call to action specifically states what the actor will do to follow up or what the actor expects the casting professional to do next. Examples of calls to action include any of the following: "I will call your office on Friday at 1 p.m. to schedule an interview," "I look forward to hearing from you," or "You can telephone me between 3 and 5 p.m. on July 12."

This call to action is a way for you, the performer, to take control of your career. If a contact number is provided, then you most certainly should mention when you will be following up on your submission. Otherwise, you might simply indicate that you look forward to either hearing from them or seeing them on the day of the audition. It is best to be assertive without being aggressive.

The second part of this final paragraph is the actor's opportunity to express gratitude for the time taken to consider her request. A quick "Thank you for your time and consideration" or "Wishing you continued success with your amazing season" or even the brief but effective "Yours truly" will all work as the thank-you of the conclusion. Keep it personal and genuine; no need to gush if you are not a gusher, yet do not hold back if you are someone who easily expresses their appreciation.

The following is an example of a conclusion (the *when*) of the standout cover letter:

> I look forward to receiving an appointment for Thursday's invited call, and thank you in advance for your careful consideration.

Done. Simple, specific, and genuine. Take a couple of minutes now to compose the "when" section of your standout cover letter.

Congratulations! You have just about completed all three parts of your very own standout cover letter. The only thing left is your signature, which you must offset with another USP moment. Find a way to show your personality in your final word(s). For example, *Best* shows that you are a person of few words, *Sincerely* demonstrates honesty and character, *Until the next* shows that you are an optimist, and *Peace* tells them that you are a nonconformist (and a really cool cat).

You might also consider using your signature as a place to show personality. In the following example, the actress abbreviates her first name to demonstrate pizazz and a sense of humor. I recommend that you play with your name to deduce which combination of names most clearly markets the "you" that you are seeking to put out there.

Putting it all together, below is our example of a standout cover letter with all of the parts combined.

TIFF ROPER

(123) 555-7890

tiffroper@abc.net

June 18, 2020

Dear Mr. Smith:

I am an experienced comedic actress with a strong command of the English language and am thrilled to submit for the role of "Beatrice" in your upcoming *Much Ado about Nothing.*

I have experience playing comedic roles such as the "Nurse" in a recent production of William Shakespeare's *Romeo and Juliet,* and worked closely with your choreographer, John Jones, who can attest to my performing skills and overall reliability.

I will be calling you on Thursday to schedule an appointment for the invited call, and thank you in advance for your time and careful consideration.

Sincerely,

Tiff

Tiffany Roper

PART IV: PROOFING YOUR STANDOUT COVER LETTER

The final portion of your job in creating your standout cover letter is finding someone to proofread it prior to sending it out. Professional casting director Chad Gracia recommends that you ask a friend to look over your standout cover letter prior to sending it off. At first, he suggests that you give it to your friend and then snatch it out of their hands after only a few seconds. Follow by asking the question, "What do you think?" See how much your friend remembers; this will tell you what parts of the letter are effective and what might need to be updated for greater impact.

Mr. Gracia insists that the standout cover letter has to fulfill three expectations: It must be *concise* (brief, compact, informational); it must be *correct* (or you will be seen as sloppy and inattentive to detail); and it must be *compelling* (again, use juicy words that will leave the reader with a real essence of who you are).

As exhausting as this may have been, you are finally done with your standout cover letter and will (hopefully) never have to do this work again (that is, until your type changes).

─────────────────○─────────────────

Compile a
Complete Rep Book

MANY TRAINING INSTITUTIONS are now striving to arm their graduates with an arsenal of reliable and well-coached audition monologues and songs that will satisfy any and all possible audition situations. The fact that, oftentimes, neither the heads of these institutions nor their individual instructors agree on the exact material that should be included in the actor's arsenal should not deter the early- and midcareer professional from working to put theirs in place. What those working in the industry know is that no two people are going to enjoy the same journey or have the same path to success. This should not keep you from putting together the best collection of audition material possible that represents you clearly while also being memorable.

My approach to preparing professionals in this area is based on practical research that I have used in my own Broadway career as well as in coaching other working professionals. I have also included some general information shared by industry friends, such as director and author Jonathan Flom (*Get the Callback*) and professional musical directors and audition accompanists Mark Akens, Howard Kilik, Andre Danek, and Brett Pontecorvo. I recommend that you use this list with a coach to help you create your own version of *your* performing artist's repertoire.

COMPILING THE MUSICAL THEATRE
PERFORMER'S REP BOOK

Before outlining the contents of what should be included in your rep book, I'd like to share a little information as to how I derived this list. Those of you with an entrepreneurial mind or a teacher's spirit might do your own similar research to further improve this list, as we all know that this is a quickly evolving industry and what is trending today will be old news in the morning.

I started this project many years ago with the May 19 issue of New York City's *Backstage*, in which I listed each and every musical theatre audition. Once listed, I began to create a system of categories that helped to combine like auditions, thereby helping me to further clarify and condense my repertoire needs (*clarify* being the key word here). I have included the initial outline in table 6.1 to help you to understand the first steps of this process.

From this research, I was able to deduce that, if I were to prepare a separate audition piece for each casting call, I would likely go crazy (and probably not prepare any of them with sufficient effort so as to make an impression). For instance, how logical would it have been for me to prepare a country ballad for the one audition and a separate country-and-western song for the other? This is probably more than apparent, but it is not so much when you consider that "Golden Age," "Traditional," and "Standard" often refer to the same genre. And depending on the pieces or your exact brand, you might also include "Legit Musical Theatre" and "Classic Legit" in this category. Also included in this category would be "Show Tune," if your voice tends to fall into less of a classical sound and more of a pop or theatrical sound.

I created the following seven combinations to help separate each potentially necessary genre:

1. Jazz Standard, Blues Standard
2. Traditional from the 1940s, Pre-Golden Age
3. Traditional, Standard Broadway, Golden Age, Legit, Show Tune, Musical Selection
4. Contemporary

5. Pop Song, Dance Club Song, Rock and Roll Song, '70s Pop Cabaret, Pop Belt
6. Folk, Country Ballad, Country and Western
7. Rock

This list is obviously a lot more manageable for someone with a busy schedule who is trying to balance auditions with showcases, commercial auditions, print go-sees, theatre- and movie-going (for

Table 6.1. List of All Musical Theatre Auditions, *Backstage*, May 19–25

Audition Type	Number of Auditions
Traditional from 1940s	1
16-Bar Selection from Golden Age	1
Standard Broadway	1
Classic Legit	1
Legit Musical Theatre That Shows Range (*Fiddler*)	1
Up-Tempo Standard Musical Theatre	1
32-Bar Comedic	1
Contemporary Musical Theatre Song	4
Contemporary Up-Tempo	1
2 Contemporary 32-Bar Cuts	1
Up-Tempo Showing Range	1
Show Tune	2
Pop/Rock	4
Pop Song Showing Range	1
Up-Tempo Pop That Shows Range	1
Up-Tempo Pop Belt	1
Short Rock Song	1
Bring Song	2
R&B	1
Dance Club Song	1
Blues Standard	1
Folk/"70s Pop/Cabaret	1
Country Western	2
Country Ballad	1
16 Bars of a Rock and Roll Song	1
'60s	1
A Cappella	1
16 Bars of a Musical Selection	1
Sing Number of Your Choice	1
Prepare a One-Minute Song	1
Total Auditions	39

research, of course), and a survival job. However, I still think that this is much too unmanageable. I have had clients tell me that they sing the same two audition songs for almost every audition, to which I say, "Bravo!" Isn't that the goal? Much like having one or two headshots, having two or three songs that work for you, that get you consistent callbacks, that you can wake up and sing whether you are sick, tired, distracted, bankrupt, whatever! That is, in all honesty, the goal.

The following is a clear example of a musical theatre performer whose rep book includes material that he enjoys, does well, and clearly markets his brand.

The Transition Workshop: The Five Repertoire Genre Categories to Compete in Today's Musical Theatre Market

Actor A (baritenor with countertenor range)
USPs: solid, quirky romantic lead, sentimental

I.   Jazz Standard

  • "Fly Me to the Moon" (Howard)—can be both romantic and quirky

II. Pre–Golden Age Musical Theatre

  • Ballad: "All the Things You Are" (Kern)
  • Up-Tempo: "This Can't Be Love" (Rodgers and Hart)

III. Traditional Musical Theatre

  • Ballad: "Come to Me, Bend to Me" (Lerner and Loewe)
  • Up-Tempo: "Something's Coming" (Bernstein and Sondheim)

IV. Contemporary Musical Theatre

  • Ballad: "Do You Remember?" (Pasek and Paul)
  • Up-Tempo: "I Could Be in Love with Someone" (Jason Robert Brown)
  • Sondheim: "Later" (Sondheim)

V.   Pop/R&B (no musical theatre; authentic pop songs by contemporary artists)

- • "This Woman's Work" (Kate Bush and Maxwell)
- • "Love Me, Love Me Not" (Joey Contreras)
- • "Do You Remember?" (Pasek and Paul)

VI.   Rock

- • None

Specialty Categories:

VII.   Operetta

- • "Oh, Is There Not One Maiden Breast" (Gilbert and Sullivan)
- • "Il Mondo Era Vuoto" (Guettel)

VIII.   Countertenor

- • "Little Bit of Good" (Kander and Ebb)

Until you get to the point where you have tested your material and know which songs consistently work for you, I recommend preparing one to two songs in each of the following categories as a way of beginning to put together your audition book.

Jazz Standard

This is a song that shows musicality, intonation, and interpretive style. Potential artists: Duke Ellington, Johnny Mercer, Hoagy Carmichael, Dorothy Fields, George and Ira Gershwin, and Fats Waller.

Pre–Golden Age Musical Theatre

This time period includes pieces ranging from the late 1800s through the 1930s. Focus on one ballad and one up-tempo piece. Potential Artists: Gilbert and Sullivan, Cole Porter, Rodgers and Hart, Kurt Weill, and Harold Arlen.

Traditional Musical Theatre

This period includes songs from c. 1940s–1960s (a.k.a., the Golden Age). Focus on one comedic and one dramatic piece. Potential artists: Comden and Green, Bernstein, latter Cole Porter, Rodgers and Hammerstein, Lerner and Loewe, and Loesser.

Contemporary Musical Theatre

This time period can range from the 1970s through the present day. Focus on one ballad and one up-tempo song. Potential artists: Stephen Schwartz, William Finn, Maltby and Shire, Ahrens and Flaherty, Craig Carnelia, Jeanine Tesori, Robert Lopez and Jeff Marx, and many others.

Pop/Rock

This category includes no musical theatre; only use authentic pop or rock songs by contemporary artists. Focus on preparing one pop and one rock, or two in each category (ballad and up-tempo).

Now, how much more manageable is this list? Are you inspired by the possibility of sifting through that huge book of thirty or more songs from your voice lessons and getting rid of most of those songs (some of which you should never have been singing anyway)?

In addition to the songs in these five categories, I also recommend that performers include material in their repertoire that supports their brand/USPs. Pieces that might do this include a vocally challenging piece, perhaps one from a Gilbert and Sullivan operetta, for those with the chops to sing difficult material. Another possibility would be a Spanish-language piece or Latino style of piece for those who would be marketable for a show by Lin-Manuel Miranda or a Latin-themed production or a show with a traditionally Latino/Latina character.

With all this in mind, the following is my list of additional "party pieces" that you should consider in compiling your audition rep book.

Specialty Categories

Operetta (Gilbert and Sullivan, Bernstein)
'50s/'60s Rock
Musical Theatre Rock (MacDermot, Ragni and Rado, Pete Townshend, Andrew Lloyd Webber)

Country/Folk
Spanish Pop (or Other Language)
R&B
Gospel
Other (Indie, Alternative, Bollywood)

Please understand that I do not recommend that you throw anything away, especially if you are either actively studying with a teacher or coach or planning on using some of this material for a future cabaret or perhaps for teaching purposes. What I recommend to performers is to keep two separate binders: one that can be used for lessons and contains all of your good and fun stuff, and the other to be strictly used as an audition binder and contains nothing but the above eight or nine pieces. Remember that anything in your book must be both performance ready and clearly market you, your talent and abilities, your vocal range, and your personality.

Another dilemma that performers often have is the challenge of selecting between two pieces in a similar genre. For example, I worked with a client who had in her book "Another Op'nin', Another Show" from the Cole Porter musical *Kiss Me, Kate* and "It's a Business" from Kander and Ebb's *Curtains*. Although one show is much more recent, both shows are written in the style of the Golden Age pieces; the characters are typical in their traditional typing and presented in very similar manners. Therefore, it did not make sense for the actress to keep both pieces in her book. How did she choose?

This is where her personal aesthetic came into play. I asked the actress the following questions: Which song shows off your voice in the best way (range, style, etc.)? Also, which song is the better acting or character/personality piece? In addition to this, which piece is less known and will make the most memorable impression? (Although I do not always agree with this statement, I have been told that there is a danger in singing material that is overdone.) Last, which song do you *love to sing*?

After asking these four questions, it usually becomes apparent to both the actress and the coach (me) which is the better piece *for her*. Sometimes it is possible to tell after singing the first three or four notes which is the better song. Remember that it is within those first few notes that you often earn your callback. Most directors can tell after the first few bars whether the actress fits a particular role in the musical. The next few bars help the director to decide if the actress is trustworthy enough to garner the callback. If your song starts slowly and warms up into a "big finish" (or, as a friend of mine calls it, "My big note!"), then it is likely not the right song for an audition. *The best audition piece will hit them fast, hit them hard, and leave them wanting more.*

For your convenience, I'm including a worksheet for you to use. Fill out your current pieces, one in each category. Remember to use what you currently have, even if you do not love it. You can always take the next couple of weeks to research independently or work with a coach to find stronger material. The key is to fill in each slot as quickly as possible to help propel you forward from struggling artist to working professional.

Worksheet: The Five Repertoire Genre Categories to Compete in Today's Musical Theatre Market

1. Jazz Standard: _____

2. Pre–Golden Age Musical Theatre (Up-Tempo and Ballad):
_____

3. Traditional Musical Theatre (Comedic and Ballad):
_____

4. Contemporary Musical Theatre (Up Tempo and Ballad):
_____

5. Pop/Rock: _____

If applicable, fill in songs for *your* "specialty categories."

1. Operetta
2. '50s/'60s Rock
3. Musical Theatre Rock
4. Country/Folk
5. Spanish Pop (or Other Language)
6. R&B
7. Gospel
8. Other (Indie, Alternative, Bollywood)

COMPILING THE ACTOR'S
MONOLOGUE REPERTOIRE COLLECTION

I must admit that I have been surprised how much more difficult and evolving this list has been in comparison with the musical theatre repertoire list. With current trends in genres that include online webisodes, as well as the increasing number of actors who now work across genres (e.g., stage, television, film, commercials, and online arenas), the following suggested repertoire list must, even more so than the previous one, be molded to fit each actor's skill level. Every actor worthy of a long-term career must consider including something from each category for their first few years of transition until they move to the stage, where they are more often than not provided sides for cold readings. Cold readings are the preferred way for directors to conduct auditions, but I still find that a solid collection of monologues is essential both in the early phase of an actor's career as well as for backup or emergency moments when a monologue is requested for reasons unknown.

Suggested monologues should be representative of each of these categories: the comedic classical monologue, the dramatic classical monologue, the comedic contemporary monologue, the dramatic contemporary monologue, the American classic monologue, the Shakespearean comedic monologue, the Shakespearean dramatic monologue, and the dialect piece. Each of these categories are briefly addressed. The following is an example of a monologue repertoire list.

The Transition Workshop:
The Working Actor's Monologue Repertoire

Actor: Melissa Ottaviano (MFA candidate, Savannah College of Art and Design)
USPs: reliable, bold and brassy, witty

- The Classical Monologue—Comedic: Diana from *All's Well That Ends Well*
- The Classical Monologue—Dramatic: Emilia from *Othello*
- The Contemporary Monologue—Comedic: Celeste from *Where's My Money* (John Patrick Shanley)

- The Contemporary Monologue—Dramatic: Sam from *Birdman or (The Unexpected Virtue of Ignorance)*
- The American Classic Monologue: TBD
- The Shakespearean Monologue—Comedic: Diana from *All's Well That Ends Well*
- The Shakespearean Monologue—Dramatic: Emilia from *Othello*
- The Dialect Piece: Italian, Janice from *Italian American Reconciliation* (John Patrick Shanley)

The Comedic Classical Monologue

When it comes to monologues, the preferred order is usually comedic, then dramatic. Yet, for some reason, actors always seem to want to do something serious first, something dramatic with lots of angst (or as Tony-winning actress Cady Huffman calls it, a "searchy" piece). Perhaps the reason behind this is that the dramatic pieces usually challenge the actor to show off his acting chops, his ability to cry, to wail, to fall on the ground and raise his voice to the stratosphere. Of course, there is great validity in selecting a piece that shows off the actor's talent, but first and foremost, the actor needs to show off the *person behind the monologue*. This is why the comedic monologue is often preferred or initially requested.

Hence, whether auditioning for a contemporary or a classical season, the standard order is to present a comedic piece first, unless the play you are auditioning specifically for is a drama. The classical comedic monologue might include a piece by such playwrights as Aristophanes and Plautus (Greek and Roman, respectively), Molière (satire/farce), and William Congreve (Restoration comedy). For those who do not often audition for classical theatre, a Shakespearean comedic monologue might also be acceptable, although Shakespeare tends to be its own category in audition settings.

The Dramatic Classical Monologue

Playwrights in this category would include Greek playwrights Aeschylus, Socrates, and Euripides; Norwegian playwright Henrik

Ibsen (*A Doll's House, Hedda Gabler, Peer Gynt*); Irish playwright George Bernard Shaw (*Major Barbara, Man and Superman*); and Russian playwright Anton Chekov (*Uncle Vanya*). The focus of the material in this category should include both heightened voice work (to include strong use of breath and diction) and a strong emotional connection to the material. Much like musical theatre, characters in the classical category, especially in the Greeks and Molière, are operating at 100 percent the entire time. This is one reason musical theatre actors often cross over into this genre for work.

The Comedic Contemporary Monologue

Once again, this tends to be the most challenging category for actors in which to locate original and appropriate material; therefore, finding that "right" piece can take quite a bit of time and a whole lot of effort. If you are not working with a monologue coach who is helping you to locate material, then you need to be doing the following: (1) reading a lot of plays, (2) seeing plenty of theatre, and (3) asking all of your theatre friends for guidance and inspiration.

The great news is that doing your research in this category should be fun. Some of the most popular plays have come from those in this category. And take heed: Although a strong comedic contemporary monologue may be hard to find, once you have that perfect monologue, it should last you for many years (and auditions) to come.

Playwrights in the comedic contemporary category include Neil Simon, whose plays from the '60s through the early '90s focus on the wear and tear of relationships in the American family. English playwright Sir Alan Ayckbourn wrote such hysterical comedies as *The Norman Conquests* and *Bedroom Farce*, which focus on deteriorating relationships. Another outstanding comedic writer is Christopher Durang, who wrote farcical comedies in the '80s and '90s that include *Beyond Therapy* and *Baby with the Bathwater*. Terrence McNally wrote compelling plays about gay life at the height of the AIDS epidemic and continues to be relevant today with *The Lisbon Traviata* and *Mothers and Sons*. And finally, playwright Paula Vogel is a Pulitzer-winning writer whose themes include such controversial issues as prostitution and sexual molestation.

This list of writers should not only assist you as a launching point to finding new and exciting material that shows off your personality, wit, and humor but also inspire you to locate other playwrights in the genre who create material for young (and those not-so-young) relevant personalities in today's stage works.

Another consideration in selecting a comedic contemporary monologue is that, for actors who do not audition with monologues very often for one reason or another—be it they do more musicals than plays or have transitioned to the point where they are called in to present sides—one of your two contemporary pieces (comedic or dramatic) be from the television or film genre. This is a great way to solve the issue of finding that perfect comedic piece, as television and film have been wrought with great funny flicks, and finding a great piece in this genre might be easier (and more fun) for many younger performers.

The Dramatic Contemporary Monologue

This is likely the easiest category in which to locate material. Hence, I simply provide a list of the top contemporary playwrights worth exploring at the beginning (or transition) of your career: Wendy Wasserstein, Nilo Cruz, Quiara Alegría Hudes, August Wilson, Suzan-Lori Parks, David Henry Hwang, Annie Baker, Stephen Adly Guirgis, Ayad Akhtar, Lynn Nottage, Eduardo Machado, Tony Kushner, and Marsha Norman.

THE AMERICAN CLASSIC MONOLOGUE

My friend, an actor and audition coach with an MFA in classical acting from American University in Washington, DC, has taught me the importance of including an American classic monologue in the rep for those who audition for regional theatre houses throughout the United States. The plays in this era, from about the 1940s to the 1980s, are considered to be a part of the Golden Age of theatre in our country; hence, much like in musical theatre, plays in this category are lauded for representing issues of importance, such as the results of war, familial dysfunction, marriage and fidelity, and other challenges of a changing America. The playwrights in American classics are known for writing compelling pieces that are both character- and action-driven. The monologues selected should also contain an element of surprise or opposites. As usual, this monologue must be type appropriate. Playwrights in this category include Tennessee Williams, William Inge, Thornton Wilder, Arthur Miller, Sam Shepard, David Mamet, and Neil Simon. Notice that Neil Simon is on both this and the comedic contemporary monologue list. Still others in this category might include Edward Albee, Eugene O'Neill, Lorraine Hansberry, Wendy Wasserstein, and August Wilson. As in the musical theatre rep list, a great way to streamline your material is to find a piece that is appropriate for two categories.

The Shakespearean Comedic Monologue

Once again, actors whose forte is not the classics may opt to combine this category with the classical comedic monologue and simply find a Shakespearean piece to satisfy both genres of audition material. Another expectation is that, if preparing two separate Shakespearean pieces, one comedic and one dramatic, at least one of the two should be a piece that is spoken in iambic pentameter (also known as verse).

In selecting and preparing your monologue, note that the best Shakespearean audition pieces demonstrate the following:

- The actor's clear understanding of the text—making certain to paraphrase the piece—is essential for clarity and interpretation
- Strong command of the language
- An ability to go from ignorance (the question or character's dilemma) to clarity (the eventual solution to the problem)
- Recognition of imagery within the piece
- Sufficient technique to *act on the text* (as opposed to *in the breath or subtext* as in contemporary theatre)

Plays within the Shakespearean comedic genre:

- *All's Well That Ends Well*
- *As You Like It*
- *The Comedy of Errors*
- *Love's Labour's Lost*
- *Measure for Measure*
- *The Merchant of Venice*
- *The Merry Wives of Windsor*
- *A Midsummer Night's Dream*
- *Much Ado about Nothing*
- *The Taming of the Shrew*
- *The Tempest*
- *Twelfth Night, or What You Will*
- *The Two Gentlemen of Verona*
- *The Winter's Tale*

The Shakespearean Dramatic Monologue

The same "rules" apply for this category as for those in Shakespeare's comedies. In addition, there are three playwrights who are sometimes considered interchangeable with Shakespeare and can be considered for variety for those professionals who wish to prepare a second piece with a slight variation: Christopher Marlowe (1564–1593), Ben Jonson (1572–1637), and Aphra Behn (1640–1689). Each of these three well-known and respected writers created pieces during the same era, and given the many controversies that surround William Shakespeare and the originality of his work, it would be quite acceptable (and often original) to offer a piece from one of the those three.

The Dialect Piece

Once again, this is a category that is easily combined with another (probably the dramatic contemporary monologue) so as to streamline your audition repertoire. The most important thing to remember is that, occasionally, directors prefer *not* to hear you do a dialect piece *unless specifically requested.* If you are not able to perform your dialect piece sans dialect, then you may wish to prepare two separate pieces.

An example of a contemporary playwright who also writes material for dialects is Martin McDonagh, whose plays' characters speak in the eastern, southwestern, and northern Irish dialects. Beth Henley creates plays about life in the southern United States with characters who are rooted in the Southern dialect. Alan Ayckbourn (also under contemporary comedic monologues) writes for those with a knack for the British dialect. And both August Wilson and Suzan-Lori Parks focus on the African American experience and create characters who speak in either traditional or poeticized black dialects.

Again, unless you are preparing for graduate school, in which a varied repertoire of audition material might be essential, as a working professional, I strongly recommend that you combine the dialect piece with one from another category to help streamline your options and allow you to focus on networking and nurturing those relationships made through the audition process.

Important note: There is a danger in working on a piece that is listed on someone's list of overdone monologues. When actors approach me with this concern, I usually advise them that, if they do the piece in their own unique way and with their own original take, as if the piece was written by that playwright expressly for them, it will not appear overdone but should have a freshness that is unexpected and will likely become a favorite for even the staunchest objector.

That said, always have a backup monologue!

Another suggestion is that you consider being an industrious and resourceful actor by piecing together a monologue that is completely original. I have often taken an extremely well-written scene and written out the scene partner's lines; in this manner, I have created a monologue that is even more conversational than most because of the author's intent of writing it as scene. And what is a monologue if not a scene with an imaginary and relatively unresponsive partner? But be ready, as your piece will likely elicit such questions as "Why did you decide to do this piece instead of such-and-such?" Your educated response to this question will not only make you seem intelligent and creatively resourceful but also give you an opportunity to display your USPs (which is, of course, the goal of the audition).

I offer this note on the topic of finding a piece that is both well written and type appropriate. Younger actors especially complain that many of the best roles are written for characters later in their lives. This is why I suggest that you research well-written scripts from both film and television to find suitable material. Today, a resourceful actor can download entire scripts online simply by typing a few key words. Still, you have to spend some time and effort researching the various scripts. However, if you have been doing your homework by watching television, films, and commercials for material (and not simply for your enjoyment), then you are already clear as to which sitcoms or nighttime episodics are in the market for someone like you or which actors have your career and which directors like working with people of your specific type. You may also be intrigued by certain movie directors, writers, or even actors and find their work compelling and worthy of exploring for this purpose as well. This, to me, is the most creative way of finding and choosing material that is original and rarely seen in an audition setting.

The second way to find material is to take monologue guru Glenn Alterman's suggestions. Mr. Alterman has written several books on finding and preparing the best audition monologues. He provides a service in which he meets with an actor and gets to know him, and follows this intensive interview with both suggested material as well as original pieces written expressly for that actor. He also suggests that, if you have a talent for writing, you consider writing your own monologue. As previously suggested, finding and working with a monologue coach is extremely recommended for those looking to transition to the next phase of their careers.

My final thought has to do with writing and performing your own audition monologue. This recommendation is highly controversial, as most industry professionals do not believe that actors should write pieces, especially ones for themselves to perform, if they have not been trained in the skill and art of writing monologues (or plays, for that matter). The danger in writing a piece for yourself is that

you will likely be so close to the material that you will be ineffec-
tive. It is like an actor also trying to direct herself; very few of us can
successfully do more than one thing at a time in this field.

However, despite the majority of naysayers, I have a Broadway
casting director friend who recently complimented a client of mine
for writing her own piece and actually recommended this as a strategy to others. I guess the moral of the story here is that, as with
any monologue, you simply cannot know if a piece will work until
you have tested it out in front of people (in other words, performed
at actual auditions). If you are getting callbacks, or at least positive
feedback, then the piece is obviously working. If not, then something has to be changed, and if you are a trained professional, then
that is usually the audition material.

Before you leave this chapter, here is your second repertoire
worksheet. As before, complete this one quickly with your current
monologues, and then research further choices in the coming weeks.

Worksheet: The Working Actor's Monologue Repertoire

1. The Classical Monologue—Comedic:

   _____

2. The Classical Monologue—Dramatic:

   _____

3. The Contemporary Monologue—Comedic:

   _____

4. The Contemporary Monologue—Dramatic:

   _____

5. The American Classic Monologue:

   _____

6. The Shakespearean Monologue—Comedic:

   _____

7. The Shakespearean Monologue—Dramatic:

   _____

8. The Dialect Piece:

   _____

——————————O——————————

Practice Preparation

ACTORS HAVE BEEN TRYING desperately to "get lucky" for a very long time. Roman dramatist and philosopher Seneca stated that "luck is when preparation meets opportunity." Although it sometimes feels as if very few people have taken his advice, Seneca warns against "trying" to get lucky but rather suggests that it is about taking the necessary steps to prepare so that, when the opportunity arrives, you are ready!

During his early days, a young Burt Reynolds asked fellow actor Clint Eastwood what he did to help himself become successful, to which Eastwood succinctly replied, "I *prepared* myself for success." This type of preparing oneself for success can take the form of many small actions. For example, do you arrive on time (i.e., ten minutes early) to each and every appointment, audition, or rehearsal? Have you found a balance between your professional career and your personal life, or do you still take rejection personally? Have you grown a thick skin so that you can cope with all of the negative and untruthful press that grows as your career grows, or does everything people say still bother you, whether or not it is the truth? Have you worked with a coach to solidify every audition song in your book so that you are ready for any request from the auditors, or are you still scrambling around last minute, looking for the perfect audition song? Are your dramatic, comedic, and classical monologues at performance level? Is your audition outfit always pressed and ready to wear at a moment's notice? Are your headshots audition ready? Is your resume specific, concise, and clear? Do you have postcards? Cover letters? Thank-you notes?

You see, there is no way around it. If you want to become successful, if you want to transition your career to the next level, then you must *take action and prepare for success*. Fame and fortune are very, very possible. But it's like winning the lottery—many can achieve it—but most of those who do win wind up losing it all because they are not ready to handle all that comes with it.

A SOLID FOUNDATION: THE MOCK AUDITION

It is essential to build a solid foundation *before* embarking on the quest for what is sure to be the next phase in your career. It will happen, if you really, really want it and are willing to work hard and take action. But will you be ready when success comes your way? You have to practice preparing for success by going through the motions of any and all types of auditions that you will encounter during your career. I call these *mock auditions*.

As casting professional Anne Teutschel advises performers, *"You must hold yourself accountable."* Do not blame others for your not getting what you say you want:

1. Take action to make it happen.
2. Prepare yourself for success by practicing (i.e., mock auditions).
3. Visualize the goal as if it has already happened.

It really works!

I was performing in Japan in a Las Vegas–style musical revue when I saw a commercial for the Broadway musical *Kiss of the Spider Woman*. At that very moment, I told myself that that was going to be my first show; I literally imagined myself as one of the guys dancing around the star in the commercial, Chita Rivera. I began to research the creative team, sought out the date of the next audition, coached my audition material, and practiced going through the motions of the audition, all the while visualizing myself dancing among those seasoned Broadway pros.

Six months later, when I finally returned to New York City, I showed up to the next open call for this musical—me and more than two hundred other hopeful male dancers. I think I was number 312! After a full day of singing and dancing, the creative team whittled it down to about ten of us, eight from an earlier invited call and two from the day's open call—I was one of these two. And I booked the job, my first national tour of a Broadway show! Of course, the next few years brought some tough lessons along the way, but my years of study, learning from others, and preparation for success solidified my reputation as a trustworthy, multitalented, and nice guy. And I've been working ever since!

"Gonna get ready" has no place in this industry. If there is anything I've learned, it is that it is not usually the most talented performer who books the job but the person who is most prepared. Take responsibility for your own luck and career. *Get ready now!*

My work as a transition coach was inspired when I was chosen to receive the inaugural Marcus Bailey and Betty Graves Shelfer Eminent Scholar Chair in Musical Theatre at Florida State University's prestigious School of Music. During my two-week residency, I taught "The Language of Fosse" through dance intensives and informal Q&A sessions. The program director and one of my mentors, Dr. Gayle Seaton, was inspirational in helping me to develop this work. Since that time, I have continued to teach master classes to early- and midcareer professionals while honing my transition strategies.

Types of Mock Auditions

Through these workshops, I have realized that the most effective method for transitioning professionals to practice their audition skills is by establishing a set of circumstances that most closely resembles those in which the performers will find themselves. This might include going through the challenging motions of the Equity principal auditions (EPA), practicing waiting with a large group at a nonunion cattle call, or setting up the environment of an absolute cold reading. The following list includes some of the more common auditions that actors go through and that I find most effective to coach, in order of practice:

1. The Basics

   • The Audition Slate
   • The Contemporary Monologue, Part 1
   • The Classical Monologue

2. The Return Auditions

   • The Successful Interview
   • The Callback

3. The Genre Auditions

   • The Musical Theatre Audition
   • The Pop Musical Audition
   • The Cold Reading/Sides
   • The Commercial Audition
   • The Film Audition
   • The Television Audition
   • The Voice-over Audition
   • The Dance Call

4. Understanding the Unions

   • The EPA (Equity Principal Audition)
   • The Equity Chorus Call

5. Final/Review

   • The Type Audition
   • The Contemporary Monologue, Part 2

These practical rehearsal auditions are called "mock auditions" and are essential to practice in front of a coach in order to analyze what the actor is *actually doing* at the audition as opposed to what they *believe* they are doing. Again, it is the most effective way for an actor to practice preparation—by actually going through the motions of each of these possible auditions.

For example, if an actor has practiced auditioning in front of people who are talking to each other while eating their smelly lunches, then the actor will not be thrown by the apparent disrespectful display to him- or herself and will still find a way to make the strongest impression possible.

The following are the most common mistakes to avoid so that you can maximize each mock audition or interview in order to practice being prepared for anything.

Four Common (Mock) Audition Mistakes

Mock auditions are the number one way in which I help clients to practice their audition skills. On the rare occasions that I am told by my clients that they are not receiving callbacks, I invite them to one of my Transition Workshops, in which I set up an actual audition setting, complete with a panel of auditors, accompanist (if a musical theatre audition), and a monitor—the works! The more I can make them relive the actual audition setting, the higher their nervousness and the more apt they are to demonstrate exactly how they *actually* audition. This is different from what they might demonstrate in a private coaching because I may be teaching in a tiny studio with a piano and small mirror—hardly the setting of most auditions.

Regardless of the level of talent, many transitioning performers tend to make some of the same mistakes without even knowing it. In fact, some of the top mistakes that performers make at auditions are oddities that have nothing to do with talent.

Mistake 1: Not Connecting

Strangely enough, what I have found is one of the most common errors that a young performer makes at an audition is that of performing the audition piece with a focus that is extremely high on the wall behind the auditors. This may seem quite inconsequential to you, but from a director's perspective, you have just knocked yourself out of the running for a callback for several reasons.

First, the director cannot connect with you if your eyes are way up in the stratosphere. Despite what your nerves may be saying to you, the director really and truly does want you to do well. However, if she cannot see and connect with you (remember USPs), if she feels that you choose to keep her from sharing in your personal journey by leaving her out (this is how it is interpreted), then you've given her no choice but to move on to the next person who will.

Having your eyes at such a high focus also tells the director that you are nervous, and this does not help her to trust you. Of course it is okay for you to be nervous, but as casting director Mark Simon advises, "Your job is to be confident and *not* show your nerves."

Therefore, I recommend that you practice setting your imaginary scene partner either directly above the center auditor's head or just left or right of the auditors. By doing so, you will not force auditors to become your scene partner while still allowing them to take the emotional journey with you. This is much more fun and a lot less stressful than beginning your monologue to a point high in the air that has no real focus, direction, or intention. Practice this strategy and watch your callback ratio increase.

Mistake 2: Performing the Wrong Material

The second big mistake that auditors make at auditions is performing the wrong material. What exactly defines *wrong*? As an actor in your early career or perhaps in your transitional stage, you do not want to remind the auditors that you either recently graduated from college or are making a transition. You need to act *as if* you have already transitioned and are confident, capable, and experienced in performing the type of role for which you are auditioning. This is a major reason I ask early professionals to delete anything on their resume that even hints of being a student. Yes, training is fine; in fact, it is necessary. But do not show them your training; show them your skill and experience.

Hence, coming in with a piece that is wrong for you is a sure sign that you are not experienced enough to know better and, therefore, will cause you to miss out on a callback even if your talent was worthy of consideration. Even if you are phenomenally talented, a professional director will not trust you if you present a piece that confuses him, but he will, instead, move on to the next person who shows that she knows who she is by performing a piece that is not only appropriate for her type but also shows her personality and other USPs.

Practicing preparation means investing in an audition coach to help you select audition material that (1) is well written, (2) is appropriate for your type, (3) shows you off well, and (4) is well coached. Every working professional knows that finding that one perfect piece takes time and a whole lot of effort. However, once you have that perfect audition monologue or song, you (and the auditors) will surely know it!

The previous chapter serves to aid you in practicing preparation by carefully selecting the perfect audition piece(s). However, you still need to hire an audition coach to help you prepare your audition pieces. I suggest that you find someone who not only assists in material selection but also works with you to create different scenarios in which to practice auditioning.

Mistake 3: Answering "No" instead of "Yes"

A third common mistake that actors make at auditions is not trusting themselves enough to answer "yes" to questions posed by the auditors. Because they have not prepared every strategy that we discuss in our earlier chapters (i.e., USPs, headshot/resume, branding, repertoire), performers often feel ill prepared and talk themselves out of a callback by answering "no" instead of "yes." Actors at auditions seem stumped when they are asked simple questions, such as "Do you have anything else?" or "Are you performing in anything at this time?" The answer to their questions always has to be some version of "yes" (we discuss this later). Yet for some reason, actors like to tell directors what they *can't do* more often than they say what they *can do*.

Here is just a sampling of the questions that I have heard actors reply in the negative to:

- Do you have something funny (or serious or classical or *anything*)? *No.*
- Do you sing pop? *No.*
- Can you tap dance? *No.*
- Have you ever worked in outdoor theatre? *No.*
- Can you read music? *No.*
- Do you know an Irish dialect? *No.*
- Anything else you want to tell me? *No, no, I said no! All I can do is my first piece and that is it!*

Obviously, the answer to many of these questions may really be "no," but this is never the right answer to give at an audition. Just like in your very first acting class, when you were not allowed to say "no" to anything but instead had to affirm "yes, and . . ." or "I'll try," so is the environment set up at the audition. Every actor must practice saying "yes" to every question that might come his way.

Imagine the difference your answer could make if, instead of answering "no" to the any of the previous questions, you said something like this:

Q: *Do you have something funny?*

A: Yes. Would you like a contemporary or classical comedic piece? (Impressive—shows you have options and are *prepared!*)

Q: *Do you sing pop?*

A: I've never been hired to do so, but I think now's my chance to start! (This demonstrates bravery and a willingness to try anything.)

Q: *Can you tap dance?*

A: I do a mean double-time step! (If not your dance skills, then your sense of humor will make an impression on them.)

Q: *Have you ever worked in outdoor theatre?*

A: I've always wanted to do outdoor theatre! (Demonstrates enthusiasm and a willingness to try anything.)

Q: *Can you read music?*

A: I hold harmonies like nobody's business and have a great ear! (Not what they asked for but exactly what they want to hear!)

Q: *Do you do an Irish dialect?*

A: I can try and also have a friend who's a great dialect coach I can work with. (Again, you have turned a *no* into a *yes!*)

You see how every possible negative answer was not only quickly diffused and turned into a positive, but this tactic also gives you the opportunity to showcase your personality and thereby cements your place in the director's memory. Even if the director decided not to call you back for lack of that particular skill, I can almost guarantee that the director will have a sense that this is a professional in front of him and worth keeping in mind for future projects.

How much more fun would it be if we all got rid of *no* from our vocabulary and simply substituted it with a more positive affirmation? I knew a Broadway actor who got a role despite not being what was originally advertised *because the actor changed the director's mind!* In fact, one of my favorite personal stories was when I attended a dance call for the role of Carl in the Broadway revival of *Bells Are Ringing*. Despite the fact that the casting notice asked for African American singer/dancers who stood 5'6" and below, I decided to show up and test my audition skills and treat it as a free class. As a 6-foot Puerto Rican actor/dancer, I obviously stood out in the crowd; and not only did I bust my butt to show that I could do what those around me could do, but I also did it in such a way that I convinced the director that I could do it better than anyone else because of my unique selling points!

Not only did I turn the casting notice from a *no* to a *yes*, but I also displayed traits that caused the director to notice me, to trust me, to alter her idea for the role to fit me, and finally *to hire me!*

And why did she do this? Because I said "yes" to everything that she asked from me and not only "yes" but also "yes, *and* . . ." Practice saying "yes, and" to every question that comes your way, and see its effect on your career as a working professional. "Yes, I'm ready for anything and am not afraid to try!"

Mistake 4: Not Taking Direction

And finally, the fourth common mistake, and the reason talented actors do not enter the realm of the working professionals, is because they have not learned the science of taking direction. My own personal experience with this came very early in my training; in fact, I wasn't even sure that my career could survive this lesson because it was extraordinarily devastating and seemed so unfair at that time.

For several months, I was preparing to audition for the lead role of Gabe in *On the Town* and did my work to prepare appropriate material along with getting coaching on it. When the audition time came, I was grounded and ready for anything—anything except for what happened. Upon presenting my audition song and reading Gabe's sides, I was asked to reread the side but to read it as if I was Chip, one of the other male leads. Then I was to reread it and perform as if I was the third male lead, Ozzie. I did what I thought the director asked me to do; however, I did not recognize that I had been preparing this role for so long and I really wanted to show that I knew who he was inside and out, and I did not veer from my original reading. My readings were not at all varied but had the same essence as my original take. I had never felt more sure of any audition and was not about to sabotage it by doing anything but the only thing that I had practiced.

Well, you know how the story ends, but can you understand why? This director told me that, although he felt that I had initially given the strongest reading for the role, it was my inability to take his direction that led him to select someone else to play the role. I had obviously practiced, but I only practiced for one thing and was not flexible on this. "How did I not take your direction?" I thought to myself and eventually said to the director. I knew what he wanted and did it on the first take. "Yes, but when I asked you to try something different, you didn't change."

Fast-forward to a few years later, and I am finally able to hear and understand what it was that he had actually been trying to tell me. What he really wanted to see was that, no matter what he would ask of me, I would trust him and follow his direction. The director needs to be able to trust his actors, and part of this is having them trust him. This lesson took me a very long time to understand because it was part of the science of practicing auditioning, and I was much too stuck on the art of portraying a role.

Hear me when I say that a strong and confident director will usually ask the actor auditioning to try something different, regardless of whether it seems right for the role. Sometimes, in fact, the director will ask the actor to try something completely opposite of what she wants just to see if the actor can take direction. Taking direction can make or break an actor at a callback, and the working professional knows this all too well and is willing to try anything because he has already practiced every scenario!

In the end, was I pissed off at my would-be director for not casting me in my dream role? You bet! Was I mad that he was trying to teach me a lesson and could have chosen a different way to teach it? Hell yeah. Was I confused for several years as to whether this was just and fair? Uh huh. Will I be forever indebted to the director for this invaluable lesson that has helped me to work nonstop for many, many years? Always—so from the bottom of my heart, John Degen, thank you.

The Mock Interview

Much like the mock audition, the mock interview is the place where the actor really gets to showcase the work ethic and personality portions of his USPs. In fact, as difficult as it is for young people to believe, this is oftentimes a more important aspect of getting the job than the actual audition portion of the work. Many a director has hired a lesser talent because they found the person to be intriguing and have that "it" quality that fit the role exactly. Talent and skill are, of course, essential to sustaining a career, but so is charisma. Therefore, showcase your personality at an interview with the understanding that this, too, is a part of your job.

Charisma comes in the form of being able to display your USPs as quickly and easily as possible each and every time you get the opportunity. Sometimes it comes in the form of the eight seconds that you get when the director asks you, "Why did you choose to do this particular piece?" Actors lose callbacks because they try to answer the question as if it were an SAT exam. No, the director does not *really* care why you did that piece; he just wants to get to know you and see if you are the type of person he wants to spend hours upon hours with in a tiny rehearsal studio. Not only does he want to know if you have the right demeanor and chemistry for the group that he is putting together but also if you are someone he might want to hang out with after hours. This is something your acting teacher may have forgotten to tell you, but chemistry is extremely important. Therefore, practice this and *really enjoy* answering the director's questions, thereby showing him how great a person you really are.

A quick note of caution: Be careful not to expend all of your energy trying to be what *they* want you to be. Many of us have stood outside the audition room, listening to discussions about what "they are looking for." The answer to this question is always tinged with a bit of "performer untruth" and tarnished by each actor's individual perspective. I admit that it took me about nine years of auditioning professionally until I finally stopped trying to be what I thought that they wanted me to be and simply just started being myself. Really? Why didn't anyone tell me this earlier? (Yeah, I know someone probably did try to tell me, but like a few of my clients, I occasionally chose to do things the hard way. That's part of the journey, I guess.)

Once I stopped trying to please everyone and started being myself, people started taking notice of me and even said things like, "I see that you've been studying. It's paying off." I wanted to say, "Sure, I've been studying—for the past ten years!" It was a great, if not long overdue, lesson for me to learn.

There's a freedom on both sides when an actor stops trying so hard and begins to trust himself in the work. But this trust doesn't just happen; it comes from lots of work and plenty of practice. Practicing in mock auditions and interviews frees the actor to know *experientially* that he is ready for every audition situation. And why is this? Because, just like a really good rehearsal, he has already practiced it!

Coda

I leave you with three additional mini-suggestions to ponder as you begin to formulate your own strategies for practicing preparation. Do not hesitate to expand your list of strategies as you continue to develop your career as a working professional:

1. *Know the players*—when it comes to knowing who will be in the audition room, do your homework!
2. *Arrive early*—well in advance of your audition time.
3. *Enjoy auditioning!*

———————○———————

Conquer
Audition Nerves

MARK SIMON, longtime Broadway casting director currently with the Los Angeles Centre Theatre Group, advises that it is okay *to be* nervous during an audition; what is not okay is *to show* the nervousness. This is a surefire way to lose the trust of people who really, really want to trust you with their work. But what does it mean to be "nervous"? What happens to us, our bodies, our minds, our abilities to produce, when we begin to feel this negative experience?

Have you ever felt your heart racing rapidly, your breathing becoming irregular, and a sense of lightheadedness? It's possible that you were feeling an overwhelming sense of *nervousness*, or maybe you were feeling the opposite, an incredible sense of *excitement*. Many dictionaries define the two, *nervousness* and *excitement*, exactly the same! Both conditions produce almost identical physical results, including a rise in physical agitation as well as an intensity of feelings. The only distinguishing marker that separates the two is the *mental interpretation* of each.

Of all of this information, perhaps most important for us to understand is not to focus on hiding the nerves, as this can often intensify the negative feelings. *Bloomberg* author Drake Bennett wrote a New Year's resolution article entitled "Feeling Nervous? Don't Try to Calm Down—Get Excited," in which he instructs us to *use* the nerves so that they work for us. Therefore, acknowledge your nerves and then work *with* them as opposed to *against* them.

Your heart races, you feel butterflies flapping wildly in your gut, your breathing intensifies, you feel a sense of heightened sensitivity, as your eyes widen and your limbs quiver with anticipation. Fear or excitement? It's both. The only difference between fear and excitement is the way you think about it.

—Tania Rose, Australian voice teacher/performer

THE SIX SUCCESSFUL STRATEGIES
FOR DEALING WITH NERVES

You're next in line, listening to another performer inside the room, wondering if you're going to remember all your words, if the accompanist is going to play too fast, if you wore the right outfit, if you warmed up enough or too much, if they're going to love you this time or hate you! You wonder if you'll get to say your name, or if you'll hyperventilate and pass out before then!

"Next!"

And away you go.

I must admit that my heart began to race as I wrote this paragraph. My breathing also became short and uneven, my focus became scattered, and I even began to shake a bit. But why did this happen to me? You would think that, after many years of going through this process, the nerves would have subsided. Heck, I wasn't even auditioning but simply *writing about auditioning*, and still I got the jitters. My own unconscious physical response to writing about auditioning is an example of the role that the mind plays in nervousness.

The nerves of auditioning and even performing can often be debilitating and prohibit us from doing our best work when it really counts. Nervousness is also occasionally a result of a fear of the unknown. Yet before we can discuss how to deal with our nerves, it is important to understand the causes of this strange yet inevitable part of the auditioning and performing process. It is imperative that we understand and acknowledge the following: *Nerves are a* normal *part of the auditioning and performing process*. Again, being nervous does not make you strange, bad, or even unprofessional—it makes you human. In fact, some experts in our field even believe that a healthy dose of nerves can be beneficial in helping to energize and inspire the performer.

Because "to be nervous" is often synonymous with possessing an unexplainable fear of the unknown, I believe that the most advantageous strategies for combatting debilitating nerves are those that help *to get rid of the "unknown."* The following six strategies help us to do just that.

Turn a Negative into a Positive

The term *nervous* has a negative connotation and usually seems to produce unwanted reactions. On the other hand, a similar yet positive term for this could possibly be the word *excitement*. By turning a negative experience ("I'm so nervous I don't know what to do.") into a positive ("I'm so excited to show them what I've prepared!"), you have changed the entire mental process, and we all know that the mind plays a strong part in the auditioning and performing process. The physical reactions may be the same, but the possibilities for joy and pleasure are increased exponentially.

During my audition workshops, I often have a monitor act as a spy by sitting outside of the audition room to observe the common mistakes made by actors. Some common mistakes reported to me are actors talking to other actors about their recent failures (i.e., reinforcing negative experiences) or performers trying to figure out what the people in the room are looking for by listening to those who complain immediately upon exiting the audition space (more negative reinforcement). To those performers who come to me for coaching, I insist on the following: Review what it is that you have to offer (i.e., your USPs), state them aloud while waiting outside the room, physicalize them, and, finally, get yourself all riled up to the point where you become *excited* about presenting this mini-performance to those inside the audition room.

Although this strategy does not help you to get rid of the unknown, it does redirect your attention onto what it is you are bringing to the audition rather than focusing on the other stuff that you cannot control. Turning the entire process into a positive is a must if you are going to succeed in this industry.

Give Yourself Permission to Fail

Actors put so much undue pressure on themselves to do well (i.e., to get the job)! Director and international educator Jonathan Flom instructs us to fight against trying to get the job, as this should not be our immediate goal. Instead, he teaches us to focus on earning a callback (*Get the Callback*, Scarecrow, 2009). Beyond this, it is important to remember that, according to Lisa Gold, professional acting/business coach, only about 20 percent of those for whom you audition will actually be looking for someone of your type. Therefore, no matter what you do, you will not get called back for at least 80 percent of your auditions.

This might sound discouraging, but hopefully it gives you a mathematical understanding of how the business works and, therefore, takes some of the pressure off you so that you can just go in and enjoy presenting your prepared material, making a new connection (or solidifying a previous one), and moving on to the next.

I encourage actors to plan on failing in some way in every audition. Expect to drop a line, choke on the high note, or even forget your name during the slate. This happens all the time to professionals of all levels. The main difference between those who earn callbacks and those who do not is that trustworthy actors don't fall apart during these moments but simply embrace them as a part of the process.

This ability to fail should help to take the pressure off you and allow you the freedom to *discover and actually have fun during the audition process*. Once you've taken this pressure off yourself, you allow yourself to relax, breathe, and do what you went there to do (i.e., *perform*)! Most casting professionals I have interacted with agree that auditioning is a strange beast, and a great many attempts have been made to reformulate how we seek out and interview potential talent. That said, keeping a sense of humor about the entire archaic process helps, too!

Practice and Prepare Way Ahead of Time

I have found that very few of us follow our own advice when it comes to this success strategy, so I'll remind us all once again: Don't wait until the opportunity presents itself to begin preparing for that opportunity! Don't wait until you receive the phone call— by then it's too late!

Prepare for the opportunity *before* it presents itself (and it *will* present itself). Practice your audition pieces at least once a week and, if possible, in front of others (a coach, teacher, or friend). This way you will have physically, mentally, and emotionally *experienced* the audition prior to it happening for real (i.e., when it counts). There really is no substitute for preparation, and this aids to decrease the feelings of fear due to the unknown.

One client of mine, Norma Perez-Hernandez, scheduled a coaching with me "for fun." She had been taking a little break from auditioning and simply wanted to sing, free of the pressure of preparing for an actual audition. It was not only a thoroughly enjoyable coaching session, but also, two weeks later, she called me to inform me that she received an invitation out of the blue to audition for a new musical. Having prepared ahead of time for this, she was able to audition with confidence and *booked the job*! Her previous practice allowed her to exude a sense of excitement and confidence. She was prepared, and it most certainly paid off.

Your grandmother's motto "Practice makes perfect" suddenly doesn't seem so cliché after all, does it?

Visualize Every Possible Scenario

When preparing a student for an audition, I use the strategy of playing their music either too quickly or much too slowly, playfully including as many wrong notes as their ears can handle. I also will occasionally quiz an actor during mock interviews in ways that make them uncomfortable in order for them to practice their improvisation skills, to help them work on thinking quickly while maintaining a sense of humor. Imagining the worst may sound pessimistic at first, but you can see how freeing this can also be.

The mission of the Transition Workshop is to allow performers to experience every possible scenario; in this way, when they encounter a similar experience, they will recall, "Oh, yeah, I've been through this already and know how to handle it." The body's cellular memory goes, "Aha! I know this!" There is freedom in familiarity. Therefore, going through the motions of mock interviews of varying types is essential in preparing the performers for success. I always recommend that actors find a coach who will help them to practice this. Improvisation classes can also be of immense help.

Visualize the worst, expect the best, and be ready for anything!

Arrive Early

There's no better way to relax at the audition space than to arrive at the space early enough to take it all in, to become acquainted with the room, to get a sense of the overall energy, to quietly and creatively prepare sides, to memorize storyboards, and so on. All of this also helps to get rid of the audition unknowns. Stage director Anne Bogart instructs actors to work with a "soft focus" (to see everything and nothing at the same time). From my studies with her, I have adapted her teachings to the audition process and have understood the value of simultaneously taking in everything—the waiting room, the "competition," the monitor, the temperature of the audition studio—that would serve me and my work.

I myself have been known to arrive *a day in advance* at the audition space, if just to "experience" the audition before the pressure of having to deliver. Becoming familiar with each audition location is essential for remaining calm and focused during this potentially stressful process. For me, arriving early simply helps me to avoid any unknowns and, again, frees me to exude excitement over what is to come!

Don't Forget to Breathe

When nervous, we tend to cut off our breathing, causing it to become shallow and disconnected, centering in the chest rather than lowering it into our backs and lower torso. This is never helpful to an actor or performer. It is important to *remind yourself* to slow down, to feel the ground underneath you, to take the weight into your legs, to allow the breath to fall down into the diaphragm at a deeper, more emotionally connected level. Anything less than this would be cheating yourself, as well as your audience.

Clinical psychologist Dr. Joshua Rosenthal reminds us to focus on the moment when all of the breath has left the body and nothing is happening. He encourages actors to breathe in for a four count, to hold the breath for a four count, and then to release the breath for a four count. This moment of stillness is the key to connecting with our true selves, the place where all creativity begins.

Recap: The Six Successful Strategies for Dealing with Nerves

1. Turn a negative into a positive.
2. Give yourself permission to fail.
3. Practice and prepare way ahead of time.
4. Visualize every possible scenario.
5. Arrive early.
6. Don't forget to breathe.

There you have them, the six successful strategies for dealing with nerves. Practice these at your next audition, and see how they diminish in importance and how they are replaced with a sense of excitement. Having practiced and prepared ahead of time, visualize every possible scenario, remember to arrive early to the audition space, connect to your body and breath, find your moment of stillness, remind yourself of your USPs, give a jump of excitement over what you have to show the auditors, and have fun!

Part III

MARKETING AND NETWORKING STRATEGIES FOR THE SUCCESSFUL PERFORMER

Success Strategy 9

—————————○—————————

Execute a
Marketing Plan

MARKETING IS ONE OF the top success strategies that each of us must master in order to maximize our visibility and opportunities as a working professional. If you really think about it, what good will it do to have mastered each of the success strategies in this book if no one out there knows that you exist? Creating a marketing plan is about getting the word out there that you exist, that you are the very best "you" on the market, and that you are available to provide your services to their all-important project! Marketing is about creating a highly visible presence, both online and through constant personal contact, so that you are on the minds of directors and casting directors at the very moment that their project is taking shape and becoming a reality.

If it sounds like a lot of work to stay in touch with every person who may be in the market for someone like you, it is. Staying relevant and on "their" minds takes constant contact, continual updates, and a visible presence at all types of theatrical events that include openings of shows, audition studios, classes, and volunteer events, just to name a few. It means sharing your thoughts and personality through the occasional Tweet with friends and fans, as well as posting updates to your Facebook fan page every day. It means sending postcards by mail to let agents know what you are currently up to, as well as to inform them that you continue to be a relevant working professional in the industry. It takes having a website with a reel of your work or photos of your album release party and visible performances easily available on YouTube and other common sites. And lastly, it means having a professional page on various casting sites where people in need of actors can find you with just a click of the browser.

Some of my students and clients embrace this success strategy a lot more easily than others. For this reason, I have compiled research as to the most effective ways to maximize your brand by creating a clear marketing plan. The more methods of contact that you give yourself to be "found" by others, the greater the probability for working and the more likely you are to continue bridging your career from just a theatre artist to a consistently working professional!

CREATING A CLEAR MARKETING PLAN

The Website

Today's working professionals have no choice but to have an online presence that makes them easy to find and follow. For the early-career professional, the *website* provides this ability in the most effective manner.

Much as we have found that a performer's USPs are essential to capture in a headshot, resume, cover letter, and other tools of the actor's trade, the website must *reinforce* the actor's brand and not confuse its audience. It must stimulate the viewer's senses with colors, textures, production stills, music, brief personal stories, and videos that reinforce the performer's talent, personality, and overall essence. I recommend that the performer include fonts and colors that already appear in her headshot, resume, and cover letter. Similar colors to the actor's eyes or clothing or a similar essence to the actor's personal brand only serves to solidify the viewer's trust in the actor and her product.

The first thing the actor must do is to decide on, and secure, the *domain name*. Most often, this is typically the first and last name of the performer followed by ".com." If the domain name is already purchased and used by another person with the same name—whether another actor, a lawyer, a dentist, or some other professional—then you need to decide on either a different industry name, add a middle initial, include a period between your first and last names, use a nickname or shortened version of your name, use ".net" or a different version instead of the more common ".com." Finally, you could go with a different name altogether. In addition, there are various companies that handle the rental of domain names, so be sure to ask your peers, teachers, and industry friends for leads on the best and most relevant hosting sites available to you. And, yes, you have to renew your membership every year, so do consider this when comparing costs of hosting sites.

Once you have purchased your domain name, it is now time to *purchase and build your website*. There are various hosting sites that are commonly used by working professionals that are relatively easy to manage and affordable to maintain. Some of the more common sites currently used by actors include Weebly.com, Wix.com, and Squarespace.com.

Keep in mind that patience is a necessary virtue when beginning to build your website. At first, the work will likely progress slowly. Building a website takes time and lots of creative energy. In addition, once everything is in place, maintenance and updates must be regular; there is nothing worse than logging on to a website and seeing yesterday's news or outdated upcoming events. Take it from me: I've made this mistake before (and, to this day, my clients do not let me forget it).

I often suggest that the working professional include no more than five separate pages or tabs, which include:

- Home
- Bio (or Biography)
- Resume
- Production Photos (or Reel)
- Contact

The actual number and names of pages will vary from one performer to the next. However, keep in mind that casting directors and other industry professionals will give you no more than two to three seconds of their time to research whether the actor is the right person for the project. For this reason, I recommend giving fewer options and more clarity from the onset. The home page will often be the "make it or break it" page, so make the most of this first page.

The Home Page

On the home page, the actor must showcase his USPs as clearly as possible. Inclusion of the actor's standard headshot and, if possible, a production photo that most clearly markets the actor is essential to have on this first and most-viewed page. The font used for the name must also showcase the performer's type and personality. I also recommend that working professionals include a pop of information, such as an upcoming project, a recent recognition ("Recently seen in *So-and-So* production"), or current goings-on ("Currently studying on-camera commercials with So-and-So"). This shows the industry professional that you are working, relevant, and active, and we all know there is nothing more attractive than a working actor!

The Biography Page

The second page, sometimes called the "Bio," "About," or "Meet" page, is the least-viewed page but one that early professionals love to include. I usually tell actors that this is the page that only their mothers will see, as it usually contains baby photos or photos from the actor's youth, as well as information as to their journey from childhood to the stage. It's a fun way for people to get to know the personality of the actor, but sometimes it's really just a fun-fact page that generally goes unnoticed by most industry professionals. That said, it is important to reiterate that every page on the actor's website must be professional; even if you post baby pictures, make sure that these are giving an impression of your personality that supports your brand.

The Resume Page

The resume page is the next important page of the professional's website. This is where talent becomes trustworthy to those in the market to hire them. For specifics on maximizing this page, please see chapter 3, as the same rules apply to the website's resume page as to the actual resume. As a reminder, the resume page must be easy to both read and maneuver. Like the actual resume, this must be constantly updated with the most current projects and information. Stale information makes the actor seem as if he or she isn't working, even though there may be new projects that simply haven't been added to the resume or website. Be certain that the resume you hand out matches the one on your website. Also, please use the tab button for all of your columns so that all of the margins align; there is nothing more frustrating to a casting professional than to have to expend additional energy trying to figure out how to match roles with locations and theatres; okay, perhaps there are other, more frustrating things, but a raggedy resume is no fun for anyone.

The Gallery/Media Page

The next page, which contains samples of the actor's work via production photos, videos, and a reel, is where the performer gets to showcase her abilities as clearly as possible. Again, please only post images and material that showcase your brand; outdated material from long ago will only confuse the viewer —this is never good. I recommend that you create subcategories for this page to include "Photos," "Videos," and "Media." Also, make certain that your reel is professionally edited and that your photos are also of a professional quality. It might be best to wait until you have a professional reel rather than posting something that is of a poor quality. If you are not satisfied that your material represents your brand in the clearest and most professional manner, then simply list "Coming Soon!" on that page. This serves as a teaser that entices the viewer to return at a later date—and then get to work on that reel!

In coaching my clients, I often recommend that they spend some time looking at videos of other actors so that they can combine their favorites into their own personal aesthetic. Some actors also hire professional videographers to do the work for them, but younger professionals are often very adept at creating their own.

The key in this, as with everything else that we explore in this handbook, is to keep the quality high and to make certain that the content clearly markets the actor's USPs.

The Contact Page

The final page is the contact page, which, once again, should have your headshot or a slightly different version that still reinforces your brand, as well as a box/area for the viewer to post a personal message if so desired. You may also wish to list your phone number on this page in case they want to contact you more quickly.

Miscellaneous Pages

I have clients who have included additional pages on their websites, including "Upcoming/News," "Reviews," and "Links." Remember that the website works best if it reinforces your USPs or brand; therefore, if it seems that an additional page or two would do this effectively, then trust your gut. I always insist to my students and clients that these are *their* careers. Take in the information provided to you as guidance, but always follow your instincts and trust yourself.

Postcards

There are various tools for marketing that are essential to the working professional. Many of these have been discussed already (e.g., headshot, resume, cover letter). However, one tool that is often forgotten is the use of the *postcard* as instrumental for staying in constant contact with industry professionals.

The two-sided postcard, either 3½ × 5 or 4¼ × 6 inches, is a relatively easy and effective way of reminding casting professionals that you exist, that you are working and in demand, that you are growing in your craft, and that you are interested in working with them on a future project. Industry professionals who have been guests at the Transition Workshop for one of my New York City studio sessions always say the same thing: Always send them regular updates with such news as recent bookings, an impressive callback, a class with a relevant industry professional, or a mutual connection made. Each of these demonstrates that you are doing your job and are reliable and worthy of a second look. Many roles are filled because the director or casting director received a breakdown for a job at the very same moment that they have a certain performer in mind. The best way to stay on someone's mind is through constant contact—the postcard is one way to do so.

Courtesy of Erin McNerney.

Courtesy of Karina Ortiz.

The actual style of the postcard varies according to the brand of the actor. However, the standard postcard (4¼ × 6 inches) features a headshot on the front and space on the back to include a short, handwritten personalized note along with the recipient's address. Make certain that your contact information appears somewhere on the card. Additionally, I have had clients stick a clear label over their headshot highlighting their most recent news (e.g., Now starring as Velma in Tri-Arts' production of *Chicago*) or a small logo of the production's poster at the bottom left corner of their headshot photo (see examples). Both of these serve to reinforce that the actor is a *working* actor worthy of consideration. And finally, the following are more samples to help inspire you.

"In the end, it is Marcos Sotomayor who owns the evening with his charismatic and charming one-man chorus character."

— NY Theatre Now —

"Reasons To Go: Marcos Sotomayor gives a stand out per-formance as a contem-porary Bronx spoken-word poet version of a Greek Chorus."

—Arts in Color—

Marcos R. Sotomayor

Courtesy of Marcos R. Sotomayor.

Marcos R. Sotomayor   marcosacts@yahoo.com

Ht: **5'9"**
Wt: **180 lbs.**
Eyes: **Brown**
Hair: **Brown**

Insert personal note here.

www.MarcosSotomayor.com

Courtesy of Marcos R. Sotomayor.

Social Media Sites

Facebook

At the time of this writing, Facebook remains the number-one way for people to remain in "personal" contact with each other. News and photos are shared with personal contacts minute by minute, almost to the point of oversaturation (and quite beyond the point of overstimulation). Professional casting directors, agents, directors, writers, and actors and performers all seem to be connected through Facebook as a way to share the most information in the fastest manner with the least amount of effort. Considering that many industry professionals now conduct business on social media, it is incredibly important for the working professional to have a Facebook page.

Some of my clients have created both a personal page and a fan page. However, I want to caution you that anything that appears on the Internet must support your brand, even if it is on your personal Facebook page. I especially advise early-career professionals to delete random silly photos of partying or other compromising situations (unless "frat guy" or "party girl" is one of your USPs). That said, the Facebook fan page allows you to separate your work persona from your personal image; you can then post friendly messages on your personal page while only posting work-related images on the other. But, again, remember that everything that is out there will be viewed and critically considered in relation to your career, especially when you are transitioning to working professional. Also, as previously stated, it takes time and effort to maintain a relevant and up-to-date online brand, so please only take on as much as you are committed to maintaining.

Twitter

In addition to Facebook, Twitter is also a relatively easy and fun way to feel as if you are in personal contact with a large number of people. Psychologically, Twitter seems to help fans to feel as if they get to have a piece of you (similar to the way that taking photos and selfies with stars does). Today's audiences are faithful to those with whom they feel intimately connected, and Twitter does this, regardless of the fact that the actor and his Twitter follower may have never even met.

Legit Actor Pages

With each passing day, there are more and more online media sites that seek to market working professionals. Some of these will outlast others, so I only list those that have been around for more than five years and consequently may continue to last beyond the initial trending phase.

IMDb

The Internet Movie Database, or IMDb, is one of the highest-regarded sites created for film professionals. Most film actors, and even some stage actors who have appeared in small movie roles, have pages dedicated to them. The accuracy of these pages is not always dependable; for this reason, some actors pay a small fee in order to update and maintain their pages themselves. With this fee comes relative control over the information that is posted, including photos, as well as the ability to delete the actor's birthdate (which the creators always post, not always in the actor's best interest).

IBDb

The stage version of IMDb is the Internet Broadway Database and works exactly the same way. Joining IBDb for the stage actor is like joining Actors' Equity Association, the professional actors' union; eventually we all have to do it, so the earlier, the better!

No-Fee Memberships Sites

Broadwayworld.com, Playbillvault.com, and Google Profiles are all legitimate websites that highlight the work of the performing arts professional for no fee. It is important to note that there are many other legitimate sites that do the same type of work, both on the local and the international level, publicizing performers as they continue to build their professional profiles. The fun thing is that inclusion on these sites is automatic once you perform your first professional job and have an established online presence. That said, the only issue that I have found is that it is difficult to maintain the accuracy of the information contained in many of the sites. As a personal example, my name has been misspelled on more jobs than I can recall; consequently, various theatrical sites like these have also misspelled my name, regardless of the fact that I have been in the business for more than fifteen years! That said, it is better to have an online presence regardless of its accuracy; there are some who insist that even bad publicity is good publicity.

Pay-to-Play Membership Sites

This is where it gets tricky. There are several membership sites that charge a fee for services rendered in addition to inclusion on their online client page. Longstanding organizations, such as Backstage .com and Actors Access, are examples of websites that post daily audition breakdowns, interviews, advertisements, and other useful and up-to-date information. In addition, they have recently included a service whereby the actor can post her headshot, resume, and profile in such a professional manner that it almost makes having a website unnecessary. I recently had a client who was asked by an agent to link onto the agency website through their Actors Access page. This "preinterview" was her first step to getting her first professional Broadway audition and eventual invitation to become a client for the agency! It is my opinion that every professional stage actor would do well to have a presence on both of these websites.

Where actors get into danger is the oversaturation of websites that deceive actors into believing that they will make them stars if they join *their* website. This used to be common mostly in the modeling industry but has recently become an extremely popular pitfall among those in the acting field as well. Many of these sites are competent at convincing the actor that membership is essential to being seen by today's industry employers, and scare tactics are often employed to nab the talent into signing a contract with the online publicity company. These online theatrical companies prey on new talent by including a few "recent" success stories as a way of tempting the performer into becoming a member, which essentially means paying a membership fee with no guarantee of actual work.

The best thing that I can recommend is to seek out working professionals within your circle and ask them of the validity of each of these sites. If it is working for someone, perhaps it is worth taking a chance and joining *for a limited time*. For example, I have had clients participate in certain showcases or join a particular publicity group when first starting out, knowing that this was more about momentum than publicity. Sometimes the reason to participate in a project, or in this case to join a website, is not necessarily for the reason that is given. Momentum is powerful in our industry. I have often said that having a "bad" agent—an agent that is not quite the perfect fit for you—is better than no agent. This is because you have to be in it to win it, and if that means joining the wrong website for a month or two until you have figured out the right website that will do the most for you, then this is another part of your business and journey to becoming a working professional. However, if you have absolutely no proof that the site that is courting you will do anything except take your money, walk on by. Although there may be no such thing as bad publicity, you should never have to pay for it! Continue spending your effort on updates to your Actors Access, Facebook, Twitter, IBDb, and the others!

Member Organizations

Additional websites that provide free publicity are those of the various performer unions. These include ActorsEquity.org and SAGAFTRA.org, which are the top two unions that professional performers must eventually join if they are, indeed, professionals. Depending on your area of expertise, you may include American Guild of Musical Artists, American Guild of Variety Artists, and possibly ProfessionalDancersSociety.org as additional options for professional unions. Some of the great perks about becoming a member of one or more of the professional performers' unions are the health and pension benefits, the union protection, contract ne-gotiation assistance, and the online presence (*more free publicity*).

Alumni Organizations

And finally, in your quest to create an online presence, inclusion in an *alumni website* for those training institutions that you attended is an essential publicity resource for those with alma maters. Many schools, as well as some teachers, coaches, and training institu-tions, are big on highlighting the work of their alumni. If you find yourself working on a project that merits exposure, I highly recom-mend that you make contact with one of the representatives from your respective university, training institution, or coach and offer to participate in a telephone interview in exchange for a shout-out in their alumni spotlight. The representative will often be more than appreciative that you have made contact (and have actually done a part of their job for them).

Be creative, proactive, and dare I say aggressive in creating and establishing your online presence. As longtime television actor Henry Winkler once advised, you must "go to work every day look-ing for work"—and establishing an online presence is a major part of that work!

Success Strategy 10

═══════════════○═══════════════

Establish Your Team

IF YOU HAVEN'T ALREADY, you will one day discover that there are plenty of people in the industry who are more than happy to bring you down and tell you that you are "not good enough." You will get plenty of opinions from industry folks and others who know absolutely nothing about our industry yet have formed strong opinions about your work. These people will gladly inform you that you are too short, too tall, not blond enough or should cut your hair, grow a beard, lose weight, get a tan, take a certain class, get a new headshot, study with so-and-so, and on and on. For this reason, it is imperative that you establish a super-strong support system—also called your *team*—who will be there to remind you of *who you really are* and what exactly it is that you have to offer. The stronger your team members, the greater your success will be. In fact, many of Hollywood's uplifting films about baseball, America's favorite pastime, focus on this (e.g., *The Bad News Bears*, *The Benchwarmers*, *Damn Yankees*).

It can also be said that striving for our best means accepting the help of others. Everyone needs a helping hand now and then, a gentle lift, or even a forceful push. If you're like me, however,

Little League philosophy: Surround yourself with a strong group of people, and you will succeed!

115

you're not all that great at asking for help and even less gracious at accepting it. Most actors tend to want to do things on their own and accomplish things through their own merits. But if you can separate your artistic self from your business self, if you can agree that you are actually a business owner and the business is *you*, then you will accept this very important part of the work.

> As a working professional, you are now the CEO of your own company, *insert your name here*, Incorporated.

It is imperative, therefore, that you work to assemble the best team possible in order to achieve your greatest results. Having people who support you and your goals is *key* to achieving success in our field. The support system is comprised of all composed the people who contribute to the development of the working actor's personal and professional life. Valorie Hubbard explores these ideas with her coauthor in *The Actor's Workbook: How to Become a Working Actor*.

> In order to optimize success, the working actor must contact each person on his or her support system every two to six months and most especially at the beginning of each transition or new journey.

Some people like to send individual e-mails; others mail out generic letters with updates. Still others I know have a monthly newsletter or send out notes of thanks every now and then. These are all excellent ways of reminding people that you are still on your quest to becoming a working professional in the industry. In addition to making contact, as each team member holds a distinct position in the actor's development as both artist and working professional, it is essential that each and every person be made aware of his or her distinct value to the artist by sending a personal note of thanks for support.

ESTABLISHING YOUR SUPPORT TEAM

Here are the areas that comprise a team, broken down into three easy-to-remember categories: personal, professional, and general support. I recommend that you fill in the name of at least one person on your personal team for each category. Note: You may use the same name more than once and may also have multiple names for each category; however, I highly recommend that you include as many team members as possible in order to maximize your outreach and potential success.

Personal Team Members

The Listener (when you just need to b*tch without judgment):

_____

The Tough Love Friend (when you know you need a kick in the rear in order to move forward): _____

The Guide (people you trust to help you get over a particular hump):

_____

The Empathetic Supporter (others in the business who know intuitively about what you are speaking):

_____

The Bigoted Supporter (member of your same gender, race, ethnicity, sexual predisposition, etc., with whom you can vent without judgment for being "wrong" or inappropriate; they know it is just a way of processing the feelings in the moment):

_____

The Nontheatrical Supporter (people not at all connected to the industry who remind you that you exist beyond the biz):

_____

Financial Supporter (people who might be able to spot you in a financial jam): _____

Professional Team Members

Talent Agents (signed or unsigned, people who deal with submissions, negotiations, mediation, buffering, etc.):

_____

Casting Directors (professional casting directors who believe in you and remind you that you are deserving of a place in the industry): _____

Directors/Choreographers/Producers/Designers/Other Actors and Performers/Etc. (established working professionals who may provide leads for getting work):

_____

Teachers (people with whom you regularly study acting, voice, dialects, dance, and movement):

_____

Audition Coaches (people who prepare you for auditions, acting/vocal coaches): _____

General Support Team Members

The Life Coach (professional in the field of problem solving):

_____

Therapist/Psychologist (professional in the field of mental health and well-being): _____

Nutritionist/Physical Fitness Coach (professional in the field of physical health, including eating disorders):

_____

Attorney (professional who deals with contracts and other legal matters): _____

Financial Planner (professional who deals with money matters with the performer's future in mind):

_____

Spiritual Support (member of clergy, church, choir, etc., who reminds you that you are OK despite any momentary challenges):

_____

Faculty Mentors (teachers who always believed in you and still do):

_____

Professional Mentor (people whose careers you want or whom you trust to guide your own career):

_____

MAKING CONTACT WITH YOUR SUPPORT TEAM

Now that you have created your list of team members, you have to take action and actually make contact with each person on your team. Don't worry—this is the easy part. Start by creating a single e-blast list with everyone on your team. Make sure to save it under "Team," as you will be using this every six to eight weeks.

Once you've set your e-blast list, *compose a very short e-mail that gives everyone specific details about where you are in your transition to becoming a working professional.* If you prefer to do something a bit more creative than a regular e-mail, you can opt to create an e-newsletter instead. This allows you to include photos, a creative heading, and other great features that showcase your USPs. Again, the option is up to you; the most important aspect is that you do this *today*—you have plenty of other work to do tomorrow, so just get it done and send it off. Actors often spend unnecessary time and energy on things that never get completed; this is why I insist on working fast and moving on to the next strategy.

Your e-mail must include the following three item details:

1. *One or two recent accomplishments* (e.g., bookings, roles performed, callbacks earned, classes completed, workshops taken, and recent meetings with industry people)
2. *One or two of your immediate goals* (e.g., taking a class, participating in an agent showcase, meeting with local casting directors)
3. *A brief thank-you* to everyone for being a part of your team and helping you to propel your career forward and achieve your goals

Important note: *Please keep it simple and brief.* In today's busy world, people don't have the luxury of reading long e-mails or newsletters, no matter how interesting the news might be to you. The key to making this first contact (and all subsequent contacts) is to be both specific and concise.

Finally, here is a sample of a brief e-blast that can be sent to everyone on a person's team. Be creative, use your own words, have a lot of fun, and enjoy the ride:

Hi all,

I apologize for the mass e-mail, but I wanted to send a quick update regarding my upcoming graduation from Manhattanville University with a BA in musical theatre. I've had four amazing years of school—just this past year, I performed the lead role of Cinderella in Stephen Sondheim's *Into the Woods* in our mainstage theatre and have finished solidifying my audition/rep book in the quest to move forward as a working professional.

I am subletting an apartment in New York City this summer and expect to participate in the May Agent Showcase at the Actors Connection. I'm beyond excited about this!

I'm thankful to you all for continuing to be a part of my support system and look forward to staying in touch!

Hoping all is well in your world,

Your name
Your phone number
Your e-mail address
Your website

Success Strategy 11

―――――○―――――

Cultivate a Mentor

THE GENESIS OF THE WORD *mentor* dates to the story of Mentor, an advisor to Telemachus and a very close friend of Odysseus, and is found in Greek mythology in Homer's *The Odyssey*. For those of you fascinated by word origins, the word *mentor* actually means "wise advisor."

A less formal and perhaps much more descriptive definition is located in Christina Katz's *The Guide for Working Moms*. In this sourcebook, *mentor* is defined as "someone who is helping you with your career, specific work projects or general life advice, out of the goodness of his or her heart." I prefer this definition because it adds an emotional component to the work, which to me is essential because the mentor's impulse is almost always a result of pure intentions and heartfelt motivation.

A mentor is a special kind of person who, sometimes unwittingly, becomes a guide to someone who is in need of something specific (e.g., direction, advice, assistance in overcoming a specific challenge, or even just a listening ear). It takes a special kind of person to become a mentor, and it is possible that person does not even know that she is a mentor. The mentor can be that third-grade teacher who took a special interest in you and helped you to see that you were special, talented, and worthy of recognition for doing a certain thing extraordinarily well (shout-out to Mrs. Roberts). Or it could be the swim team coach who pushed you to strive for your very best even though you never even wanted to be on a team sport and hated the water (yeah, those were some rough years). Mentors teach us lessons that live on with us for many years and guide us through some of life's toughest challenges.

In the case of a struggling artist who aspires to become a working professional, an industry mentor is that person who gently guides your career by listening, asking questions, encouraging, and motivating you to take action toward achieving the next phase of your success. Having a mentor is similar to working with a manager, only mentors work for free! Mentors are, for some inexplicable reason, extremely attached to the goal of seeing you succeed; at times, they may even seem to want this to happen more than you do. Their generosity of spirit (and time, energy, etc.) is curious perhaps, but a mentor is a special type of person whom no dreamer—or aspiring working professional—should be without.

THE ART AND SCIENCE OF FINDING
AND CONNECTING TO A MENTOR

What Makes a Good Mentor?

What are the traits that make a good mentor? *Experience!* Experience in the arts demonstrates an ability to struggle through very difficult circumstances and thrive despite enduring the hard knocks of aiming for success in our field. Sometimes the mentor's personal experiences teach the mentee how to progress in the industry without having to endure the same types of challenges that the mentor had to sustain and eventually overcome.

Some areas in our industry in which I have helped to connect clients to mentors have been with professionals in casting, directing, and producing. Casting mentors often expose the apprentice to the inner workings of the business (e.g., answering phone calls and e-mails, scheduling audition appointments, and serving as a reader for actual auditions). The directing mentor might welcome the observer to participate in the creative process from a very different perspective (i.e., behind the table). And a producer might expose the mentee to the world of negotiating contracts and even offer an opportunity to participate in the high-pressure realities of producing theatre.

Examples of invaluable lessons that an industry hopeful might encounter under such mentors include:

• Never put your own money into a production.
• Ninety percent of good directing is in casting the right people in the right roles.
• Always negotiate a contract *in writing!*

Imagine the many other tidbits of invaluable insights that a reputable industry mentor could offer to an up-and-coming talent!

A Mentor Makes Things Possible

Another reason successful working professionals take advantage of their relationships with industry mentors is because *the mentor exemplifies what is possible and attainable*; if the mentor can do it, then so can I! The mentor represents what is possible in our industry.

When I was in undergraduate school, little did my classmates and I know that within our group were future Tony Award–winning producers, Tony-nominated actors, and performers in Tony Award–winning productions. At first, it felt as if we had to forge our own way, but we also proved to those graduating after us that a career in the industry was not only possible but also expected—*success was their destiny*. Our musical theatre program's strong belief in mentoring the next generation of professionals is intrinsic to the program and instrumental to the students' transition and overall success.

Depending on where you are in your career and what your goal is for your next transition, I provide a list of prospective mentors for you to consider later in this chapter.

Industry Mentors: Who Are They and How Do I Get One?

I want to pause a moment to remind us that the primary goal of this book is to offer business strategies for becoming a *working professional*. A working professional is a businessman or -woman who is earning a living in the performing arts. With this in mind, I highly recommend exploring the *Forbes* magazine's May 17, 2013, issue, which offers an inspirational article by Jacquelyn Smith entitled "How to Be a Great Mentor." In it, she interviews career coach and star of MTV's *Hired* Ryan Kahn. She also offers nine strategies for those who desire to become mentors themselves. In its simplest form, a mentor is someone who imparts wisdom and shares knowledge. To me, it is most important that the mentor *inspires you to become the very best* you.

David Parnell, legal consultant and communication coach, advises would-be mentors, "One should give back at least what they've received." And another leader in the field of giving back is Dave Ramsey, financial advisor, who is known to give free tuition to attend his financial literacy program to couples in need of a beacon of light in the storm. In return, the couples must promise to give the same gift of free tuition to another couple in need when they finally become free from debt.

The following are characteristics that I consider essential for a mentor to possess:

- A mentor *recommends* teachers, coaches, and other necessary team members (such as tax accountants, lawyers, etc.) to you when you are in need of very specific guidance.
- A mentor *refers* you to his contacts (directors looking for talent, choreographers seeking assistants for preproduction, producers seeking driven production assistants).
- A mentor *listens* to you without judgement following a difficult audition or related experience.
- A mentor *asks* the right questions to help you figure out how to move forward with a certain goal/objective.
- A mentor *helps* with goal setting and outlining strategies for achieving those goals.
- A mentor *counsels* you to help you move beyond and reach your next level of success.
- A mentor *shares* personal experiences and learns from the personal experiences of others in order to help you to not feel alone on your journey.

- A mentor *provides* you the space to be able to experience your lesson on your own.
- A mentor *inspires* you to define and fulfill your dreams!

There you have it—the mentor *recommends, refers, listens, asks, helps, counsels, shares, provides, and, most important, inspires!*

What a Mentor Does *Not* Do

There are some other traits that you may find in a mentor that I would caution you against accepting. Be wary if you encounter any of these traits or actions in a potential industry mentor.

Gives You Advice on Relationships

As much as an industry mentor may genuinely care about your personal and mental health and stability, they understand that they are not qualified to give such advice that would be better left to the trained psychologist and relationship expert. There is a line that the mentor does not cross with someone to whom they are providing nurturing guidance; the power imbalance must be respected by maintaining clear boundaries throughout the relationship.

Tells You How to Live Your Life

I must admit that I learned this lesson partway through my work as a college professor. One of my students with whom I was working as an industry mentor made the decision to quit school during her junior year to participate in an off Broadway production in which she got to work with a reputable director. I was not in favor of her decision, as I was looking at the long-term repercussions of what her decision would mean at such a sensitive point in her studies. In the end, it was I who learned the more valuable lesson. The student taught me that I had crossed that invisible line and reminded me that it was her life she was living and not mine. Ouch! She taught me an invaluable lesson that has since helped me to better guide others. In the end, she ultimately returned to school immediately following the production and completed her degree, so we both got what we wanted in the end but not without having learned a valuable lesson on space and boundaries.

Disagrees with Your Parents and Close Friends and Dismisses Their Opinions as Uninformed, Regardless of Their Knowledge of the Industry

Once again, the mentor must respect that there are boundaries in her relationship with the mentee; giving her opinion on the mentee's family life and dissenting points of view is inappropriate, no matter how much the mentor wishes to be supportive to the mentee. The mentor must always respect the family's perspective, even if she disagrees with it.

Takes You Out on a Date

Ever heard of the infamous casting couch? One would think that this was a thing of the past. Perhaps it is not as overt and openly accepted as it once was (Was it ever okay?), but it certainly does still exist. For more on this, see the casting director's interview later in this chapter.

Babysits

If there is no apparent forward movement in the actor's career, the mentor will not continue to invest time and effort into the relationship. The legitimate industry professional values his time and does not provide a warning to the performer—the mentor simply moves on to someone else who values his knowledge and career guidance.

Selecting a Mentor

So now that you know what a mentor does and does not do, as well as what to look for in a suitable mentor, the following are some of the potential industry mentors who are available to you:

• Alumni
• Casting directors

- Agents
- Directors
- Choreographers
- Producers
- Vocal coaches
- Audition accompanists
- Acting instructors
- Company managers
- Designers
- Other actors

Erin McNerney and Danyel Fulton, AEA actresses and working professionals, recommend formulating close relationships with dance teachers, voice instructors, and acting coaches. These are the usual suspects when it comes to potential industry mentors, as they have the most personal attachment to the working professional and his or her career.

In addition, for some reason, actors would never think to consider an audition accompanist to be available to them as an industry mentor. However, I have had many clients make strong connections with accompanists who also work regularly playing for auditions. They offered what many would consider secret insights into the audition process, as well as what to expect from different directors and casting directors. In my early years of auditioning, I recall making a connection with an audition accompanist who was also serving as a Broadway rehearsal accompanist. He stopped me on my way out of the audition room and mentioned that I demonstrated strong audition skills and that I would certainly make an impact on the casting director of his show. I immediately began preparing myself for that opportunity! You never know where your next connection will come from; if you create a bond with an audition accompanist, be open to the possibilities of a mentor–mentee relationship.

Another unexpected mentor–mentee relationship, perhaps, can evolve with a working designer. Everyone knows that my favorite place to be when performing in a show is in the costume shop. Hanging out with the folks in the costume and hair departments brings me joy no matter how exhausting a production might be (yes, theatre is work). Designers are known to have favorites among actors with whom they enjoy working and for whom they revel in designing, and are occasionally open to guiding these actors through the navigation of their next transition in the industry. Therefore, do your homework, know *all* the players, be gracious, and stay alert—you never know who your next mentor will be.

Considering Alumni

Yes, it is true that the two most common potential mentors exist in the student–coach relationship and in the alliance between the agent and the client. That said, I also believe that a strong bond, as well as some solid guidance to maneuver the industry's ups and downs, can evolve from building a relationship with alumni from the mentee's alma mater.

Begin by doing your research on the alumni from your alma mater who are also working professionally in your chosen industry. College graduates with something in common can be your number-one resource for transitioning your career to the next level. Most universities have alumni associations that might be able to help you to get in touch with a potential mentor. These potential mentors can be instrumental in helping to answer your questions, creating a roadmap of potential strategies, further supplementing your connections, and even serving as overall industry guides.

Although the alumni association and alumni magazines are resources for tracking working alums, you should also track the success of your university's graduates independently and find a way to make contact with them while you are still a student. Students can be industrious by creating school projects that include an outreach component. During my master's studies at Penn State, I devised a project in which my cast of undergraduate students had to make contact with twenty-five working Broadway performers. As part of their work, they were expected to conduct a short interview with each of them; some chose to do this online, while others received permission to contact them by telephone. One student actually traveled to New York City and conducted the interview in person.

Each of the twenty-five performers was eager to respond to the students' requests and was more than happy to participate in our creative project. In the end, this opened the students' imaginations to the possibilities that were available to them and to the people who were waiting to help them after graduation. With this example, I recommend that you talk to your college instructors, alumni association coordinator, and even other students to strategize ways of making contact with a graduate whose career most closely resembles the one that you have visualized for yourself.

The Casting Director Is Your Friend

In addition to alumni, in closing, I recommend formulating a relationship with each and every casting director who has expressed a desire to be a part of your team. Any casting director for whom you have auditioned more than once is likely an excellent candidate for an industry mentor. Some of my most genuine relationships that were filled with caring and insightful conversations were with prominent casting directors. There is a mutual respect that working professionals in the industry garner for each other; they understand that we all need each other in order to continue working professionally. It has been my experience that the casting director epitomizes this essence.

I was fortunate throughout my performing career to maintain a positive reputation as someone who was reliable, passionate, a hard worker, and an overall nice guy; these traits made me a favorite among casting directors, and they would often share industry secrets and casting strategies with me because they genuinely wanted to see me succeed.

If you are a stage actor, research all of the casting directors who work with stage actors, and begin to nurture relationships with them. This information can be found in the seasonal *Casting Call* as well as other resources (contact the Drama Book Shop in New York City for guidance). All you have to do is plant a seed by making an introduction, sending a two-sentence e-mail requesting ten minutes of their time, and follow up with a thank-you note. I have had clients travel to Los Angeles to meet with several of my casting director friends out there as a way of getting to know the LA industry. They would invite the casting director out for coffee or a quick lunch in exchange for a tête-á-tête to discuss industry strategies as well as to make a new connection. If you are lucky, the casting director will invite you to an industry mixer and even submit you for an audition. This is not very common, but it does occur. Yet despite all of the extras that can result from that initial meeting, having had a one-to-one with a working casting director provides you with invaluable information and personal strategies for becoming a working professional in the industry.

An Interview with Casting Associate Jeffrey Drew, Los Angeles, California

At the time of this writing, Jeffrey was casting *Dallas*, *Chuck*, and several other television shows and pilots.

JULIO AGUSTIN (JA): I am completing my chapter on the importance of transitioning professionals' connecting with potential mentors in the industry. Can you discuss some of the work that you do that you feel goes beyond your work as a casting director in Los Angeles?

JEFFREY DREW (JD): I teach many workshops for actors auditioning for casting directors. I do this throughout the year as a way of passing on information. The most important thing that I try to get across to young hopefuls is that their job is just *to keep showing up*, as well as *to bring their authentic self*—you can't be anyone other than who you are.

JA: And what is it that drives you to go above and beyond for the talent in LA?

JD: Actors need to feel supported. They don't talk about the auditions that they are not getting [the number of auditions that they go to that they don't book]. Actors need to share this so that they know they're all in the same boat. There's no shame in not booking; that's a major part of your job and journey as a working professional.

JA: What type of actor makes the strongest impression on you, and how exactly do you mentor them?

JD: Yes, I have taken people on who are new to the area and possess what I believe to be star quality. I see someone and believe in their talent. This can happen at a workshop, in a yoga class, on a Facebook exchange, anywhere. Sometimes their talent and its endless possibilities get muddy, convoluted by bad choices and habits. I try to give them encouragement and work with them to get them on track. I also often work with them on their cold reading skills.

JA: And what exactly do you offer them?

JD: I try to strip it all down to the basics. Oftentimes we meet at Starbucks (six shots, iced espresso in a venti cup!) and go through sides together. We also discuss the industry and how it really works. *It's about doing a good job more than about getting the job.* This is tough for them to understand, but if they stay in it, it eventually makes sense.

JA: How about the issue of boundaries? Do you believe that the infamous casting couch still exists in today's industry?

JD: I don't believe in crossing boundaries. And yes, the casting couch still exists—people are still inappropriately crossing boundaries—but it happens from both sides. When I transitioned from acting professionally to casting full time, I was warned about being "sprayed down" by actors in the industry. The beautiful ones use their currency (good looks, sexuality, whatever) to try to get seen. It's important to always stay aware of this and maintain your boundaries.

JA: Thank you, Jeffrey, for your candid discussion. I am sure many will find it extremely helpful—if not entertaining!

The Mentor Worksheet

From the list of potential mentors mentioned in this chapter, select three people whom you could most easily contact *today*:

_____

_____

_____

Select two additional people with whom you will make contact in the next week (seven days):

_____

_____

Choose four additional people (from different categories or the same), and write their names down. Research their contact information. Consider making contact with them when you have exhausted your relationship with the previous three prospective mentors:

_____

_____

_____

_____

On a final note, one of my favorite mentoring stories involves an actress whom I coached for several years and who transitioned from early-career performer to working professional. Now a member of the three actor unions (SAG, AFTRA, and most recently AEA), she has been working on television, was a lead singer on a Disney ship, has performed principal roles in regional productions, and is very close to booking her first production contract.

I received an e-mail from a previous college professor of hers who knew that I worked with her as an industry mentor. He had received an inquiry from a director wanting to know about her abilities to handle comedy, as well as her overall work ethic and reputation. As her mentor, I was happy to contact the director and give my perspective on her abilities and potential for success in the industry (which she had already proved). The director contacted me right away and thanked me for my candid response and helpful remarks.

The actress was brought back in by that director for a final callback and contacted me afterward to mention that my name was brought up during her meeting. Her exact words to me were, "My ears are burning. Have you been talking about me?" I mentioned that I had been contacted for a reference, not by the director, but by the director's industry contact. It is almost unbelievable how many people are involved in helping to propel a person's career forward. Needless to say Jasmine Romero booked the job—another lead role with a working director who is also an up-and-coming brilliant talent.

And that, my friends, is how powerful (and necessary) a relationship with a mentor is!

Get "Them"
to Trust You

As in any professional industry that invests hundreds of thousands, if not millions, of dollars into a product, a director, producer, or casting director is not often going to hire someone about whom they know practically nothing. No matter how amazingly talented a performer shows herself to be during her audition, very few people hire an unknown these days.

I know of a singer/dancer who moved to New York City after many years of working regionally. He auditioned extremely well, often earning callbacks, and was kept to the very end of each audition. Yet he was having a difficult time breaking in to the New York City theatre community because he had not yet worked with anyone in town. Even though he received continuous positive feedback from casting directors, he wasn't booking anything.

As you read this, I am guessing that many of you can relate to his story, especially if you are in your first two years as a professional. After so many great auditions and with so much positive feedback, the actor was beginning to think that the business was just not for him and seriously contemplated a move back to his hometown.

He recalled leaving another callback just as deflated as he could be and walking to a nearby payphone on the corner (yes, this was quite a few years ago), where he called his parents and told them that he was coming home. A couple of days later, he received a letter in the mail from one of the Broadway directors for whom he had just had a callback. It was just like in the movies! No, it wasn't an offer, but almost. It was a personal note stating that the actor had made a great impression at his audition, but that the project had fallen through; however, he was definitely on the radar of this director. Because of this, the actor decided not to go home after all; instead, he took the note as encouragement to press onward and to never give up!

This performer eventually booked his first national tour and, a little later, because of his excellent reputation while on the road, had his Broadway debut in a show directed by the director who had sent the letter years ago. After what seemed like years of final callbacks with this director, he was finally cast in his first Broadway show. He had gotten the director to trust him via his skill, reputation, and connections.

If you haven't already guessed it, that young man was *me!* Not only had I been diligent in clearly marketing my USPs—tenacious, comedic dancer/actor, really nice guy—but I also had repeatedly proven this to everyone over and over until they trusted me and my work. Not only have I seen the USPs in action, but I also have lived it!

Another more recent example of getting someone to trust them was recounted by Bernard Telsey, owner of one of New York City's most prestigious casting agencies, Telsey and Co. He spoke at a seminar for aspiring actors and recounted that he actually requested a written reference about a particular actress prior to casting her in the national tour of *Porgy and Bess*. He requested information that had to do with not only her abilities but also her timeliness and other personality traits that might affect her ability to get along with her coworkers. Reputation does matter!

Let's look at this yet another way: Ask yourself when the last time was that you got a haircut. Do you remember how it was that you found your hairstylist? Was it by recommendation from someone whose opinion you trusted? Or did you just do a walk-in to any random salon or barber shop? And if for some reason you did so and received a terrible chop, did you return?

Most people wouldn't trust their hair to just anyone. Nor would they trust their teeth to just any dentist or their skin to just any skin product. Not even cars are entrusted to just any mechanic or repairman. Think about it: Would you take your car to just any mechanic for service? Or rather, do you not ask your friends and relatives for recommendations before entrusting someone with such a valuable asset?

Even though we all know that our hair will grow back, most of us think twice before trusting an "unknown" with our hair. So how could you possibly expect a playwright, director, or producer to trust their million-dollar project to someone about whom they know absolutely nothing? *Unless they know you or someone who knows you, they are not going to take a chance on you.* Furthermore, unlike your hair, their money will probably not grow back.

Three Key Points on the Subject of Trust

1. In order for them to trust you, they must *believe* that they know you.
2. People trust people they know.
3. The key is to figure out ways of getting known.

The following are some ideas and actions that we explore in the quest to getting auditors to trust us.

STRATEGIES FOR GETTING THEM TO TRUST YOU

People Trust People They've Seen

The next best thing to having worked with a particular director is to *get seen* by that particular director (or casting director, agent, etc.). Work begets work, which is why working professionals surround themselves with people who are working and do as many projects as humanly possible in order to keep the momentum going.

Industry people are constantly attending showcases, readings, workshops, cabarets, and one-man/-woman shows. It is a well-known fact among working professionals that industry folk send representatives or assistants to projects they themselves cannot attend.

As part of my duties during my stint as a university musical theatre program coordinator, I served as the director and facilitator of the annual New York City Industry Showcase. One of my main goals was to invite agents and casting directors to attend the showcase. My strategy included inviting not only the agency heads but also their associates and interns. I knew that our best bet would be to get an associate to attend and consider the talent onstage, which several did. These industry assistants and associates would, in turn, go back to the agency and submit their list of candidates to the agency head for their consideration. And, voilà, that is how the students of the university received offers for meetings, auditions, and even representation!

At the beginning of your career, or even your career in transition, you have to be resourceful to create projects whereby you can showcase your talents. Some venues to consider include the industry showcase, off-off Broadway, and student films.

Industry Showcase

In larger cities like New York, Los Angeles, Chicago, and Washington, DC, there are now companies that put together showcases of varying types (singing, acting, comedy, even complete productions). The best ones are those that guarantee an audience of industry professionals. These showcases will cost you, so be certain to do your homework and ask such questions as who attended the previous showcase and what percentage of performers got signed.

Off-Off-Broadway

The thing about an off-off-Broadway production is that there are no union regulations, so a talented performer can commit her time and talents to a project in exchange for publicity. Of course, you want to make sure that your work in the piece, if not the entire production, is a quality performance and worthy of inviting industry professionals. Industry professionals often forgive a truly bad production if they are able to discover a new or unrepresented talent. Do not feel badly for inviting them; just make sure that you pay for their ticket and that your work is exquisite.

Student Films

Many large cities have excellent film departments that early-career actors can contact and commit their time and talents to in exchange for copies of the work for their reels.

People Trust References

Of all industry professionals, casting directors are known to be the most actor friendly; they often invite their favorite actors to the auditions on which they are working in the hopes of seeing them book the role. Casting directors have a reputation for really liking actors and caring about their careers. They are, perhaps, the most nurturing people in the industry. I recall with great respect one of my mentors, Vinnie Liff, longtime co-owner and casting director of the Johnson-Liff Casting Office. Vinnie (as he was affectionately known in the industry) actually called me to offer me my first Broadway production rather than contacting my agent and having him give me the call. His phone call made me wonder who was more excited: me at booking the job or him for being able to deliver the good news. This was my first of many experiences in which I got to see the joy that casting directors get in being able to bring talented performers closer to their dreams. The casting director's job is to connect those providing the work with those who are look-ing for work and able to deliver the goods. For this reason, I highly recommend to you, as an artist looking to become a working profes-sional, to get to know your casting directors and other people who will eventually serve as references for you.

Other important resources you might also consider as references are directors with whom you've worked, other actors who know your work, and friends and family members who have a connection to someone in the industry. This is where spreading a wide net is essen-tial. Go back and refine success strategy 10, "Establish Your Team," and think about six degrees of separation; you already know someone who knows someone who knows the person whom you need to know!

After the casting director, the agent is probably the next person whom a performing artist needs to focus on adding to their team. Longtime talent agent Dave Bennett insists that getting someone to recommend you is arguably the *best* way of getting seen for a gig. If you are doing a showcase or some other production, make it your business to get to know those actors in the production who have an agent, and when the time is right, ask them if they would consider recommending you to their agent (another reason to be kind to everyone). Agents, directors, choreographers—they all believe in references and are more apt to hire you if someone with whom you have already worked puts her reputation on the line for you.

People Trust Their Connections

This is similar to references, except that connections do not get you in the door through a reference but simply by way of their own reputation. In other words, usually naming a person whom you and the auditors have in common gives them a sense that you deserve a second look (i.e., a callback). You should always research everyone involved in the project for which you wish to audition as a way of finding your "in." For example, do you know someone who has already worked for this director or production company? Or maybe they have seen something that you were in? Have they taught a workshop at your alma mater? Any of these can get you to stand out, thereby engendering trust in you by way of your connections.

Your resume is your greatest and most likely tool for accomplishing this. This is why you need to create the clearest, most powerful resume possible (see success strategy 3, "Create a Captivating Resume"). In fact, this is the real reason people list recognizable names on their resumes. It is one of the simplest and most effective strategies that artists often miss, so do not hesitate to use your contacts as references for attaining work.

In addition, listing other mutual connectors (such as being in one of the actor unions, studying with a reputable teacher, or having graduated from a mutual alma mater) is an excellent strategy for establishing a connection with those behind the audition table.

Trust = Volunteering

Actor and audition coach Aaron Galligan-Stierle teaches that there are only three reasons for accepting a job in our industry:

1. The job provides you with monetary payment for your service and skill.
2. The job offers you an opportunity to perform a role for creative or resume-building purposes.
3. The job provides you with the opportunity to network.

He also states that, if you are fortunate enough to get two out of three of these, then you are a very lucky person. With this in mind, I often help clients to strategize ways in which to volunteer to achieve numbers 2 and 3 on this list. In the performing arts industry, volunteering can come in many forms, such as working with a choreographer on the preproduction aspect of the show or assisting the musical director with such tasks as copies, binding, and so on, or even in performing such jobs as ticket taker, usher, bartender/ caterer, photographer, distributor, PR person, and many more. In fact, in New York City and other major theatre hubs, working for free is part of paying your dues. Therefore, finding ways to immerse yourself in the industry is essential, and volunteering provides a great way of achieving this.

A quick word of warning: Working in these types of jobs must be dealt with carefully because being seen in these service positions will sometimes do more harm than good. That said, if all of those involved understand and are clear that you are an actor first but also want to help the creative team in a service capacity, then you have clarified your goals from the very beginning and may actually be considered for a performance spot when the timing is right.

One of the greatest careers that I can think of that started out through the act of love and service is that of Tony Award–winning director Jerry Mitchell. Mr. Mitchell's enthusiasm and ingenuity in creating a benefit to raise money for those stricken with the AIDS epidemic evolved from a handful of dancers to what is now an annual event of more than one hundred performers that has raised millions of dollars for Broadway Cares/Equity Fights AIDS. *Broadway Bares* was, perhaps in a large part, the springboard that led to his transition from chorus dancer to now-legendary choreographer and director. He has since given countless opportunities to hundreds of would-be Broadway dreamers like myself to volunteer to sing and dance (albeit mostly in the nude) in front of hundreds of audience members with handfuls of cash. Like Mr. Mitchell, *Broadway Bares* never takes itself too seriously while still taking the mission of the work very seriously. It is also an excellent example of a venue that has provided opportunities for performers to make the connections that have propelled their careers to the next level.

> Volunteering allows you to build good karma, forces you to acknowledge and appreciate your own good fortune, and just plain feels good.

On a final note, understand that everyone has to pay their dues. This seems especially difficult for artists to understand because they believe that they have something special to share with the world and are often impatient to do so. Still, paying your dues is often an important part of the journey in the entertainment industry; it also gives us some entertaining war stories to share later in our careers! You have to believe that every famous person has had to pay his or her dues; it's just a part of the field that you have chosen. Your job is simply to continue planting the seeds that build your reputation as a trustworthy professional.

Stand firm in the knowledge that, although getting that first job in the industry is often a catch-22, the theatre community of working professionals is an extremely small one. As you continue to take steps to establish yourself as a working professional, you are essentially planting seeds with each and every audition and connection that you make. All you need is that first job—once you are in, *you are in!*

Success Strategy 13

───────────────○───────────────

Network!

PROFESSIONAL ACTOR AND AUDITION coach Aaron Galligan-Stierle once said that he believes an actor can call himself a professional when one or more of the following is true: There is financial compensation for the work, he is booked for a role that will enhance his resume and lead to more work, and there is the opportunity to work with someone in the industry who can enhance his life as an artist or professional. Aaron also reminded me that, if the actor is able to achieve two out of three of these, he should not only consider himself a professional actor but also a *very lucky* professional actor!

As a professional actor or performer, of course we want to get paid for our work. However, it is important for the young actor and those transitioning in the business to understand that the first three years as a full-time/transitioning professional performer focus on numbers 2 and 3 of this list—enhancing the resume and making connections (i.e., networking). This is what is meant by "paying your dues."

Before we discuss the whos, wheres, and hows of networking, let us clearly understand what exactly it is that proper networking can do for an actor and her career. Networking can help a professional actor:

- Learn about auditions
- Meet people who are "in the know" of the latest industry information

- Find a sublet or place to live
- Prepare for auditions
- Receive recommendations for a good acting coach, accountant, or sideline job, among others
- Get recommended as a last-minute replacement for an acting job
- Get called to an invited audition
- Recommend you to take their place in a job because they just booked another one

And on and on!

What you need to understand is that networking is one of the most powerful tools, not only in the performing arts, but also in any industry. Some people waste so much time trying to figure things out on their own rather than relying on their support system (and their support system's network) for guidance and assistance in propelling their careers forward.

> The three most important things in this industry are talent, hard work, and connections—but not necessarily in that order!

THE WHO, WHERE, AND HOW OF NETWORKING

The *Who* of Networking

Perhaps the easiest of the three to understand is the who of networking. Who are the connections in this industry with whom we should become acquainted? The answer: *Anyone who is connected to any aspect of the performing arts is a connection.* This would include not only the obvious—agents, casting directors, directors, choreographers, and other working actors—but also those in other theatrical positions that are somehow connected to the performing arts. Some such examples are the stage door concierge (useful for dropping off notes and learning the ins and outs of the backstage world), the box office manager (who always knows of free tickets to performances and might add you to their e-blast list), the company manager (who deals with contracts, negotiations, money), the acting instructor (who is always well connected), the receptionist at the dance studio (who knows who is teaching and which classes might be more appropriate for you), the hairdresser who is married to the Broadway performer, and so on. Anyone remotely connected with the industry will one day serve as a contact for you, just as you will serve as a contact for them.

For example, I cannot tell you how many times I have been contacted by someone who knows someone who knows me who was trying to get tickets to a show in which I knew someone who knew someone who was in the show. This six degrees of separation often guaranteed them house seats for the Broadway show of their choice! And that, my friends, is one of the many benefits of establishing a healthy network.

It bears repeating that the concept of six degrees of separation is more than a theory originally proposed by a Hungarian writer in 1929. It has been tried out by countless people in countless professions with proven success. In his book *The Power of Who: You Already Know Everyone You Need to Know*, Bob Beaudine gives detailed strategies for nurturing your current network, as well as expanding your team to include people who are on your team's team. He instructs his readers to involve those currently in their network (e.g., friends, family members, work colleagues) as a way of expanding their network in any specific direction. For example, if I were seeking a television audition coach, rather than proceed blindly through the many listings on Google or another source, I would be better off to request references from my friends and colleagues. In this manner, I have involved the support of others, which has saved me both valuable time and energy. This is a fascinating theory and worth the time and energy to investigate.

Last, anyone who attended college has a neat little network of friends for life that has been built into their degrees in the form of an alumni association. Not only does just about every university in the country have a network set up to help connect those recent and not-so-recent graduates, but also often each department (e.g., theatre, music, film and media production) has immediate access to those in the area who might serve as contacts for those from the same alma mater. For example, the Florida State University's music and theatre departments are known to invite each and every music and theatre alumni, as well as their industry guests (e.g., agents, managers) to their annual New York City showcase. This outreach has been proven to maximize the number of the new graduates who are instantly embraced by industry folk, further proving that the university alumni networks work!

I want to add a word of caution as you move forward to increase your network of industry contacts: *Never, ever, ever burn a bridge!* Just as there are six degrees of separation in *building* a solid team of contacts, a bad experience with someone can also *destroy* your reputation. This is an industry that takes a lot of time, energy, and money to rectify a negative reputation. Although sometimes challenging, this is a business in which it is best to keep your nose clean and your opinions to yourself.

The *Where* of Networking

Where exactly do you go to connect with people who might be important in the industry? If you live in a metropolitan city like New York City, Chicago, DC, Miami, or Los Angeles, then the answer is *everywhere!*

Everyone in LA knows that you don't leave the house without being "show ready." This means hair done, clothes pressed, shoes (or flip-flops) shined, and face ready for action. When living there, I used to find it unnerving that, upon entering a restaurant, bar, or coffee shop, everyone would turn around to see who it was walking through the door! This, I later learned, was pretty standard, as everyone who is anyone in LA is always show ready. People in Los Angeles understand that working there is about seeing and being seen—it's all about networking.

Another delightful experience about living in a metropolitan city is the way one can obtain work. In New York City, it is not uncommon to meet people on the subway who will actually connect you with work. I once met a working playwright who was doing a reading, who asked me to participate in his project. So the next time you are traveling on the subway, at a restaurant, or on a busy street, stay alive, alert, and *show ready!*

Every metropolitan city has its own unique networking system. It is important to spend some time figuring this out—it is your job to understand how the industry works in your neck of the woods. In my opinion, a working professional expects to expand her connections each and every time she walks out of her apartment, condo, beach house, or wherever she resides. It is important to be *ready for anything*, or, as Henry Winkler once said, to "go to work every day looking for work."

Besides the generic answer of "network everywhere," other more specific locations where actors can network, regardless of the size of the city, are such audition centers as the Actors' Equity offices in your city and the SAG and AFTRA membership buildings, as well as performance venues, like movie theatres and live stages. Even the music and drama sections of the local bookstore and library can lead to expanding your network. It is never a bad idea to spend some quality time frequenting these locations, if just for the dual purposes of meeting people and finding out the latest industry news.

The *How* of Networking (or How to Avoid Kissing A**)

It is not uncommon for me to coach an actor who has great reservations about putting himself out there to see and be seen, to meet people, to "schmooze," in essence, to network. Yet he may, unfortunately, view the networking part of the work as the seedier cousin, kissing butt. So what exactly is the difference between the two?

In success strategy 8, "Conquer Audition Nerves," we explored the major difference between being *nervous* and being *excited* as a matter of perspective. In a similar manner, it is the same with networking versus kissing butt; the greatest difference is in perspective and approach. In essence, there is a negative way of looking at this aspect of the industry; that is, having to talk with people whom you don't really know or truly care about or feeling disingenuous, as if you are trying to be nice to these people for the sole purpose of getting work.

On the other hand, you can choose to look at it from another perspective, a more positive approach that includes

- Meeting new and exciting people
- Learning about yourself and others in the industry
- Discovering how connections work in this profession
- Talking about yourself as a way of exploring who you are or have become
- Recognizing how your talents and skills are most useful to people in the industry
- Expanding your team and support system
- Cementing your position as a working professional in the industry

Can you, in all honesty, find anything wrong with any of these? It's all a matter of perspective, and as a working professional, you have to embrace this aspect of the career if you wish to continue to develop as a working professional.

The following strategies were sent to me from industry professionals; use these to develop your own networking strategies:

- Regularly keep track of people's social media presence. Stay informed by knowing about people's latest projects.
- Stay in touch. If you are on their mind (and in their message box) at the time of a casting, then you may be the person who gets the job!
- Nurture your relationship with assistants, interns, and so on. Today's assistant is tomorrow's head casting director!
- Get to know other actors' work, especially those you respect, by regularly attending their performances. They may, in turn, get to know you and take an interest in your career.
- When in conversation, always have a talking point that does not relate to theatre or the business.
- Try to embrace the need to network, understanding that everyone is there for the same reason.
- Smile. Be friendly and inviting.
- Be genuine. People can smell a fake from a mile away!
- Attend workshops and other networking opportunities.

- Nurture the contacts that you make at auditions, classes, and voice lessons.
- Get out! Hang out with people. Most of your work at first may just be through recommendations by those with whom you are hanging out.
- Stay connected through cards, e-mails, and so on, but don't get aggressive. Respect people's privacy.
- Take notes at auditions, workshops, and so on. You need to remember the people you meet if you expect them to remember you.
- Alert casting directors and others when you are going out of town for work. Not only will they be grateful for the update, but they will also perceive that you are a working professional, which makes you that much more valuable.
- Bonus: Understand that some people you may have networked with will become lifelong friends!

In conclusion, I asked three of my clients, all professional actresses, to weigh in on the topic. They had the following advice to add to the conversation: Comedienne Casey Miko recommends, "Strike up a conversation, be pleasant, and just be yourself." Actor/singer Danyel Fulton says, "Because we can't predict the future, we can't assume that our fears will come true. And who cares? Take the risk to be open, friendly, and genuine, and you may just be shocked by all of the new contacts that you've made along the way just by taking the risk." And actor/singer/dancer Erin McNerney advises, "Get over yourself! Yes, networking is scary, but it's necessary. Period."

Success Strategy 14

---○---

Follow Up for Superior Results

READY TO TAKE an industry quiz?

Quiz: The Follow-Up

1. *Who* should I follow up with?
2. *What* should I follow up with?
3. *When* should I follow up?
4. *Where* can I find the contact information in order to follow up?
5. *Why* should I follow up?

Extra Credit: *How* should I follow up?

THE *WHO*, *WHAT*, *WHEN*, *WHERE*, *WHY*, AND *HOW* OF FOLLOWING UP

Who Should I Follow Up With?

Staying connected can often feel like a full-time job. Unless you have an agent and a publicist keeping your name floating about, it is imperative for the professional performer to send occasional updates to everyone with whom he has previously worked in order to keep propelling his career forward.

People Who Should Receive a Regular Follow-Up

- Directors familiar with your work
- Casting directors for whom you have auditioned
- Artistic directors who have hired you before
- Teachers with an active connection to the industry
- Agents, managers, or other industry representatives with whom you are trying to build a relationship
- Anyone whose name appears on your resume

It is my experience that actors focus predominantly on establishing connections with agents and directors. And yet, very few early-career professionals understand that the *casting directors* are their greatest resource and liaison to those directors. By nature of the casting director's work, most of them appreciate actors and even take great pride in being a part of their ongoing careers. In fact, many casting directors began their careers as actors themselves and so are empathetic to the emotional roller coaster that actors must go through in this industry. They take great pride in seeing their "favorites" booked!

Casting directors see hundreds of actors at every audition; unfortunately, many report that a large number of those auditioning are often grossly underprepared and leave a negative imprint on their overall audition. This is why casting directors often become personally invested in the actor who shows herself to be reliable and completely prepared. Respect for the casting director's work is essential, and you can do this by demonstrating that you are a trustworthy working professional who is both reliable and prepared.

Artistic directors are another group of people who prefer to work with the same handful of actors; therefore, getting them to know your work could prove extremely beneficial for your career. You can start doing this by researching the type of productions that the company in question tends to produce. You can also demonstrate reliability by learning the type of audience that the theatre serves. Last, knowing the names of the people (actors, directors, etc.) who work steadily at the theatre is essential to getting in with the company. And if you can also find out something personal about the artistic director that might link you to her and her work, this could also be a great asset to you.

Some of our greatest team members are our current and previous *instructors*, especially those who maintain an active relationship with those in the industry. Although I know that many actors feel uncomfortable asking for recommendations from their teachers and coaches, you should never feel this way. Most teachers are more than happy to help propel your career forward in whatever way possible. In fact, they have dedicated their lives to this purpose, so take advantage of it!

The list of people with whom you should follow up also includes agents, managers, audition studio owners, and so on—basically anyone who is connected to the industry is someone with whom you should regularly follow up. Most important, do not forget to contact everyone whose name appears on your resume. They appear on your resume because they are working professionals with a certain amount of credibility; if they are not recognizable industry professionals or up-and-coming creative artists, then perhaps they should not appear on your resume to begin with. Unless you are a younger actor, do not clutter your resume with the name of your Dover Junior High School teacher who directs the annual school play unless she is also a professional director during her summer breaks. Also avoid listing your peers' names unless they are aggressively pursuing a directing or casting career and you expect this contact to be relevant as you move your career forward.

That said, anyone with whom you have worked and whose name appears on your resume is an industry contact and must receive a regular follow-up in order to help you maximize your potential for becoming a working professional.

What Should I Follow Up With?

The most traditional manner of following up with industry professionals is to send either a personal thank-you note, a picture postcard, a flyer from a showcase or other performance project, or, when available, an updated headshot and resume. If you have created an online relationship with the person, then you may also send a thank-you e-mail that contains your business signature as well as your headshot at the bottom, along with a headshot and resume as an attachment.

The follow-up is a very personal matter and should be handled in the manner that most closely expresses who you are. Many people today feel that they are being disingenuous if they send a personal thank-you note in the mail; still others love making contact and often hand-create their personal cards. It really is a personal matter and should definitely support your USPs. For example, if you are marketing someone who is professional, regal, and down to earth, then your method of contact will be much more on the professional side than someone whose brand includes such characteristics as enthusiastic, bubbly, and nice. It is *you* that you are marketing, so keep it personal and authentic.

In addition, as with everything in this industry, keep the contact brief. The note should include a simple thank-you (for the recent audition, etc.), as well as a sentence about what you are doing (e.g., "I recently booked a national commercial for Tide detergent"). That is all. Do not say, "I hope to see you again soon," or anything of that nature; it is understood that you are hopeful to reconnect and are keeping them abreast of your goings-on. They will appreciate the update, especially when they are casting something for which you would be perfect.

Please do not bypass this success strategy. Actors believe that they are one of a kind and will be remembered for months after their audition. However, Kurt Stamm, artistic director of the Mason Street Warehouse, informed me that he receives hundreds of headshots for each project that he produces. Therefore, those actors who are in contact with him on a regular basis are more apt to receive an invitation for a project.

Staying in touch takes time and a whole lot of effort, but this is also an important part of the working professional's job, so *just do it!*

When Should I Follow Up?

The follow-up postcard (thank-you card, etc.) must be sent at one of three times: immediately following every audition, every six to eight weeks, or every time there is something new to report. News worth reporting may include a recent booking (hooray!), an upcoming performance (offer them comp tickets!), a major callback, a class taken with a reputable industry contact, and even a new connection made through one of these. You must be tenacious yet also sensitive to the fact that they are busy professionals; please do not send a card "just to say hello," as this will surely turn them off to you.

I directed a production in which I had an actress who did an OK job during the audition but whom I did not find all that interesting. After the audition, I received a generous thank-you note in the mail, which I mentally filed. A couple of months later, I received a postcard update from her. I also received an e-mail informing me that she was participating in workshops as well as taking classes with industry professionals, all the while auditioning full time. Because my coaching career took off, I never got the chance to call her in for anything again, but believe me, if I had another project for which I could have called her in, I certainly would have. She made an extremely strong impression on me, if not necessarily because of her talent, but for the fact that she was doing everything that a working professional would do and she had *earned* my trust.

Reminding industry folk that you have both the persistence and the intuitive ability to do everything that it takes to be a professional in this industry makes a great impact on the psyches of those in the market to hire you. As previously stated, casting directors often speak of the hundreds of performers that they see on a daily basis who arrive unprepared and are ill equipped to be given any real consideration. Therefore, when they encounter someone who maintains regular contact and is doing all of the right things (working, receiving callbacks, studying, and not giving up), the performer is undoubtedly leaps and bounds ahead of those who may feel entitled to the same consideration for simply showing up. The six- to eight-week updates help you to build your industry reputation and trust factor.

Where Can I Find the Contact Information in Order to Follow Up?

Research the industry person's contact information, making certain to include the correct spelling of the person's name as well as the proper mailing address. Also, seek out the appropriate title for each person in the office, as you do not want to call an associate an assistant, for example. In today's digital world, there is no excuse for errors in spelling or location.

Contact information can easily be located by doing a Google search, but you must also confirm accuracy by placing a quick call to the office. It is perfectly acceptable to telephone the agency, state your name clearly, and request confirmation of the information by reciting it as concisely as possible. In fact, you might think of this as yet another opportunity to make contact. Do not feel that you are doing something inappropriate or unethical—this is part of your job as a working professional. Always identify yourself and your reason for calling when confirming information. Be polite, and keep it very, very brief.

Why Should I Follow Up?

Why am I insisting that you add to your transition strategies something that requires so much effort? I contend that this is essential because, in this industry, the saying "Out of sight, out of mind" really and truly does apply. People in the performing arts lead extremely hectic lives, such that timing is a major factor in achieving success. This is especially where the term *luck* becomes a factor.

Luck can be defined as the moment when preparation meets opportunity, and opportunity is a matter of timing. Therefore, by consistently placing your materials in front of industry professionals when they are actively working on projects and in need of filling spots, your effort will surely pay off.

I cannot tell you how many of my clients have received auditions and, consequently, work because I was in contact with a director at the very same moment that the director was in need of an actor like the one I was presently coaching. In fact, a large percentage of performers get hired not because of having initially auditioned for a role but because they were lucky enough to have their materials in front of someone at the perfect time.

People hire people whom they know and trust, and putting yourself in front of them over and over gives them the sense that they know you and can therefore trust your professionalism and talent. For this reason, it is important to stay connected with your growing network because you never know when your follow-up material and a casting opportunity will intersect.

Make no mistake: Casting people see hundreds, if not thousands, of people weekly and *will forget anyone who is not right in front of them* (even if only in the form of a picture postcard). Monthly contacts with brief updates keep you in people's minds and make you a trusted entity.

How Should I Follow Up?

This final note is one of the most important aspects of following up early and often. Knowing exactly *how* an industry professional wishes to be contacted—whether by e-mail, snail mail, telephone, or social media—and following explicit directions is essential in proving yourself a reliable talent worth considering. I have seen performers lose out on work because they did not follow simple contact instructions. In fact, I once had a client who lost out on a meeting with an agent with whom I had set her up because she did not follow his instructions. The agent wanted her to mail her materials and write across the front of the envelope "referred by Julio Agustin." Several weeks later, I touched base with the agent to see why he had not contacted my client, only to learn that he never received her package. I was obviously confused and a bit distraught that I had put my name behind someone who did not follow through. However, my client insisted that she had sent her materials to him—*by e-mail!*

Unfortunately, she learned a very difficult lesson by sending the e-mail instead of the hard copy by mail. The agent's assistant receives hundreds of e-mails every day and must have obviously deleted hers with the bunch. Had my client followed directions, the assistant would have, first of all, had to handle the envelope, and second, he would have seen the "referred by" instructions across the envelope, thereby guaranteeing her a shot at an interview.

Be sure to read the small print when you are following up with industry professionals. Some prefer hard copies sent to them in the mail, while others might be okay with e-mail contacts. Still others approve of hand-delivered items (another way for them to actually see you). It all depends on each individual, so again, do your research so that you do not risk upsetting the very people you are trying to impress.

In my opinion, it is usually most effective to mail the follow-up material via U.S. mail. This ensures that someone in the office has to physically handle the envelope and do something with it. I have often been advised that e-mailing material, unless specifically requested, is a bad idea. Many offices receive more than two hundred e-mails a day, which greatly increases your chances of having your material deleted. Do not take the risk—send it in the mail.

COMMITTING TO FOLLOWING THROUGH

Special Hints: Now that you have committed to *following up* with everyone who has the potential of propelling your career forward and helping you to establish yourself as a working professional, I also want you to make the commitment to *follow through* by doing the following.

1. Do What You Say You Can Do

Following through simply means doing what you say you are going to do. If you say you are a singer, then you better have your audition repertoire book ready for any request that may be made of you. You also better be able to pick up music fairly quickly, hold your vocal part, and, of course, sing really well.

Talent agent Jed Abrahams says that the entertainment industries in big cities like New York and Los Angeles are for performers who are experts in their field. They are not for people who do something kind of OK; it is for the best of the best. The worst thing that you can do is list something on your resume that you do not do with great proficiency. Therefore, do what you say you can do, and do it really, really well.

2. Showing Up Is 80 Percent of Booking the Job

Every Equity performer knows how common it is for people to sign up for an Equity chorus audition and not show up. You might be number 207 on the sign-up sheet and wind up auditioning as number 50 on the actual audition day because of the number of people who could not be bothered to show up (e.g., worked late, broke up with a boyfriend, lost his phone, alarm did not go off). This is a common issue among performers, both nonunion and union, so make it a habit to increase your odds by following through and showing up, even if you have a legitimate reason for not doing so. You will be surprised how often this works in your favor.

3. Do Less, and Do It Well

Another common mistake performers make is double-booking themselves. It is an infraction that can have devastating results to one's reputation. Do not audition for something during a time when you are already doing something else. If you do, then you may gain the reputation of someone who is in demand but also not trustworthy—the worst kind of reputation.

I know of an actor who was working on a movie at the same time that he was on hold for a national commercial. An offer for the commercial came, and as is Murphy's Law, it overlapped with the film shoot *by one day!* This actor received calls from the ad agency, the casting director, and his own agent threatening to sue him for not fulfilling his agreement. He tried to get out of his film contract, but by that point, many of the scenes had been filmed and consistency was on the line. Needless to say, he never worked for either the commercial casting director or the movie director again!

Yes, I know, here I go again contradicting myself. Although I regularly tell actors to audition for everything as a way of practicing their craft, I also strongly advise them against double-booking themselves. Understand that, if you are offered a contract that you do not accept, you will likely burn that bridge. This is one of the most difficult lessons for young performers who have received their training from institutions where they were involved in several projects simultaneously. It is never a good thing to teach that you can be two places at one time. You simply cannot be! This is a business in which your reputation precedes you, so *please* do not say "yes" to more than one project at a time. Your future may depend on it.

4. Underpromise and Overdeliver

Author and coach Talane Miedaner recommends that you underpromise and overdeliver in your business. Do more than you say you can do, or do it better than you say you can do it. This is, again, one of the most commonly experienced letdowns. People's resumes list special skills that, when asked to produce, are often performed at the basic and not mastery level. If you say you can do something, then *follow through*, and do it better than anyone else out there!

Remember that quiz you took at the very beginning of the chapter? Take a few minutes now to complete your own list of connections and resources that will allow you to take immediate action.

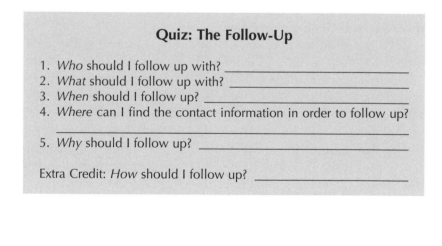

Quiz: The Follow-Up

1. *Who* should I follow up with? _____
2. *What* should I follow up with? _____
3. *When* should I follow up? _____
4. *Where* can I find the contact information in order to follow up?
   _____
5. *Why* should I follow up? _____

Extra Credit: *How* should I follow up? _____

Part IV

OFFSTAGE AND
PROFESSIONALIZATION
STRATEGIES

Success Strategy 15

─────────────○─────────────

Organize Your
Home Office

PRACTICALLY EVERY ACTOR hopes to have an agent or a manager working for them, keeping them organized, helping them get to the next level. Yet because the average agent gets paid 10 percent of an actor's salary for their work, it is expected that the actor is responsible for the remaining 90 percent of his career. By now you know that that's a lot of "stuff" to keep straight in managing your career—train schedules, audition studio locations, catering jobs, agent appointments, acting classes, drop-offs at the cleaners, mending holes in tights, visiting Granny on the way back home—the list is endless. In order to handle the demands of running your company, you have to be able to manage each and every aspect of your career with a clear head, superior juggling skill, and the grace of a swan (or dancer). The ability to keep such a hectic schedule requires an immense talent for organization, both while at home and on the go.

In order to do all of this, I insist that a professional must establish a safe environment in which to create and maintain her business. Therefore, as the CEO of You, Incorporated, you must create an organized workspace that supports your ability to grow and maintain your career. And you do this by *creating and organizing your home office*. You must also put together what is commonly known as the "go bag" that ensures you are prepared for any and every possible audition situation.

Every single working professional must set up a home office that is clean, organized, and contains all of the necessary business tools to sustain a busy career in the performing arts. Items that belong in this space include the obvious tools of the trade (headshots and resumes, thank-you cards, perhaps a calendar or day planner) as well as things that might seem inconsequential but are still very necessary (paper clips, stapler, hole puncher, etc.). Until you are at the point where you are able to hire a press agent to manage your career, you have to maintain an organized space that supports your hectic lifestyle, a space that is conducive to growing opportunities as they continue to roll in (and they will). A designated home office workspace is essential in supporting this goal and helping you transition to the next level of your career.

The size of your office is not important; in fact, even *a small desk with filing cabinet* will suffice as long as this area is used exclusively for the purpose of growing your acting career. Please do not use your office desk as a coffee table or file your cable bills among those in your work files (unless your cable is part of your business, in which case, file on). Separate your professional work from your personal and any other business matters. You must compartmentalize your performance work in order to keep from clouding it with matters from your personal life and vice versa.

In addition, do not combine your performing business with any other sideline work that you have created for yourself. If you are a performer *and* a web designer, then I suggest that you maintain separate areas for each type of work (e.g., separate resumes, separate contacts, and separate areas of the office). As you already know, this is an industry that insists on type casting; therefore, if you brand yourself as a comedic actor who dances, you would not want to cloud your image by branding yourself as someone who also builds websites. If you do that type of work, then make sure that you market it separately. This also goes for those of you who choreograph or direct or stage manage. Keep each of your brands distinct by creating a separate resume from that of your acting resume. Do not mix performance work with that of directing, choreographing, stage managing, costume designing, publicity consulting, production assisting, and the like. Your early acting career must never get mixed up with your other professional work; this intermingling can confuse those in the industry and may, in fact, make them less apt to trust you in either field.

THE MAKINGS OF THE HOME OFFICE

The three nonnegotiable items that you need for your home office are *a desk, a chair*, and *a filing cabinet*. The desk serves as your work area, where you keep a computer in order to respond to e-mail submissions, create and send standout cover letters, update your website, revise your resume, and conduct other similar work. This area also serves as your work station, where you can write your postcards and thank-you notes and address envelopes. You should also consider investing in a small printer; a scanner and fax machine may be useful as well.

In addition to the desk, you need to invest in a comfortable (although not too comfortable) chair, bench, or stool in which to sit while doing your work. Please do not spend a lot of money on this; all you need is to make sure the chair is solid and supports your back so that you can maintain your posture and energy while completing tasks.

The final component of your home office is the filing cabinet. Our industry has evolved to the point that things now happen at lightning speed. You can expect to make dozens of important industry connections daily. If you are doing your job, you will be running from your day job to an afternoon audition to classes at night and then to a callback the very next day. In between all of this, you will be submitting yourself for auditions, responding to e-mails, writing and mailing thank-you notes, recording the details of your last audition, filing your receipts, budgeting for the week, ironing your audition clothes, preparing the next day's lunch, and tackling many other tasks that require excellent organizational skills. As you can see, you will be going back and forth from your desk to your files to manage your career. Therefore, an organized workspace is nonnegotiable—you have to set up your home office!

WHAT BELONGS ON YOUR DESK
(AND IN YOUR FILING CABINET)

As a working professional, you must keep every receipt for items purchased and file these away in order to itemize your expenditures. Some people keep a small accordion file in which they throw their receipts and ultimately file them once a week, month, or year. Others, like myself, prefer to dump them all into a container and simply go through them once a year. Either way works; the important thing is to keep them safely filed so that you can get the greatest write-off at the end of the year.

As an actor, you are considered an independent contractor. You are the CEO of your own company. And much like the entrepreneur who opens and runs her own small business, almost every aspect of running your own business is tax deductible. You must keep your receipts so that you can prove this on your annual income tax report. In essence, if you have not already done so, set up your bin for storing receipts today. Details on what is considered a write-off are provided later in this chapter.

In closing this portion of the strategy on organization, I recommend that you keep either a bamboo plant, a photo of your favorite niece, or an inspirational article on your desk in order to add just a bit of Zen to your work station. A picture (of children or a spouse, preferably yours) could also be nice, as long as you remember that this is your *work* station and should serve to inspire you to continue your evolution as a working professional. Anything that might distract you should *not* be a part of this area. If you want to earn respect in this industry, then you must begin by treating your home office with the same type of respect.

THE "GO BAG"

"go bag" (n.): a bag packed with essential items and kept ready for use in the event of an emergency evacuation of one's home

The Home Office: The Basics

Easily accessible:

- Receipt file
- Audition planner
- Stapler
- Hole puncher
- Paper clips
- Pens
- Pencil and sharpener

Drawers:

- Stack of twelve primary headshots with resumes attached
- Stack of headshots and resumes (not attached)
- Secondary headshots
- Zed/composite cards (for those who do commercial print work)
- Thank-you cards
- Business cards and postcards
- Blank envelopes, return address stickers, and postage stamps
- Large manila envelopes (for mailing headshots and resumes)
- Show programs
- DVDs of recorded work
- Miscellaneous items

Files:

- Correspondence (mailed and e-mailed submissions for work)
- Contact sheets from each show (for future reference)
- Tax and accounting information
- Annual receipts (you may file your receipts here)

As previously discussed, aside from always carrying your headshots, resumes, audition book, and now audition log and journal to each audition, there are several other items that you do not want to leave behind. Some of these are specific to certain types of auditions (for example, dance shoes for dance auditions), but once you set this piece of the actor's puzzle up, it requires minimal upkeep.

You can always recognize a dancer at auditions because theirs is the heaviest "go bag"! If you expect to book work as a dancer, then your dance shoes better always travel with you, even if the audition does not specify that a dance combination will be taught. Most musical theatre performers can attest to having attended a singer call in which they were surprised to find that they had to dance, too! A dancer is always ready for anything (including a dry change of clothing), so never leave home without these.

Ladies should have character shoes with the industry standard 2½-inch heel. But please make sure you have previously worked in your shoes, and do not wear something that throws you off balance. I borrowed my roommate's flamenco shoes once for a major Broadway audition. I figured that the shoes would give me a longer, sleeker line and a bit more height. Well, I moved like a twelve-year-old in her first pair of heels—bent knees and all. Not cute! I have seen women do this all the time, borrow each other's shoes. If you borrow shoes, then make sure that you have practiced in them, or you may be surprised, and not in a good way.

Additional items to include in your "go bag": aspirin (or ibuprofen), throat lozenges, hair ties and hair pins, breath mints, bottled water, a simple snack (granola bar, trail mix, fruit), and a phone charger are must-haves for when you are stuck at an audition for hours at a time. Suggested (but not required) items include a small stapler, pen, pencil, and pencil sharpener. Not all of these are necessary for every audition, but most will be used in your lifetime auditioning as a working professional.

Don't forget to also carry a small towel and reapplication of makeup. If you are auditioning regularly, then you will be running from one audition to the next with very little time to freshen up. Even though you are living the life of a gypsy, you are still expected to look fabulous for each and every audition. Therefore, bringing a bag of hair and makeup products to freshen up is essential, both for women as well as for men. Every male actor should invest in a small compact of pressed, translucent powder. Your standard drugstore sells these, although MAC makeup also carries them in various shades for matching skin tone. That said, men must be careful not to appear made up unless this is part of your USPs. The objective is to get rid of the unflattering shine, not to look made up. This shine is particularly unattractive in on-camera auditions.

And finally, one of the most essential tools that I insist all actors carry with them at all times is the *audition journal* (also known as the Holdon log; see table 15.1). The audition journal functions in two ways. First, the business portion of this journal helps you to keep a log of the specifics of each and every one of your auditions. You want to keep a record of the names of each and every person who was at your audition (including the accompanist and monitor); the date, time, location, and project for which you were auditioning; the names of the pieces that you performed; a detailed list of the exact clothing that you wore; and any comments that were made regarding your audition ("nice job," "good song for you," "callback!"). All of this serves you in the following ways: First, if you receive a callback, you will want to perform the exact same audition pieces, wear the exact same outfit, and perform as close to the same way as possible. If you made a good impression on them the first time, then why change anything? Second, your log serves as a record for possible future auditions, meetings, and so on. Occasionally, you will receive a phone call a year later regarding an audition that you did the year before. The audition log helps to remind you of the details of that audition so that you can review what worked and prepare for this next audition or interview accordingly.

A word about callbacks: If the auditors liked what they saw enough to give you a second shot at it, then why on earth would you even *think* that it is OK to alter any of it? There are stories of people being called back for shows and then losing the job because they wore something different or performed a different audition piece, causing the people behind the table to feel as if the person whom they called back neglected to show up. For this reason, you must believe me: If it worked once, then do it again!

There is a great book by my good friend Jonathan Flom entitled *Get the Callback* that gives more detailed information on understanding auditions and callbacks. In it, he emphasizes that the callback should be a less stressful audition because you have already proven that you are "right" for the role. Once you get a callback, it really is out of your hands; for this reason, you should find

Table 15.1.   Sample Audition Log

Date:	_____
Project:	_____
Role:	_____
Director:	_____
Casting Director:	_____
Casting Assistant:	_____
Producers:	_____
Monitor:	_____
Writer:	_____
Composer and Lyricist:	_____
Musical Director:	_____
Choreographer:	_____
Time:	_____
Location:	_____
Personal Info:	_____
Audition Material Performed:	_____
Alternate Audition Piece:	_____
Audition Attire:	_____
Audition Assessment:	_____
Callback Information:	_____
Other Impressions:	_____

a way to relax and allow your personality to shine and have fun. At that point, it's all about whether you fit the costume or if you have the right chemistry to be combined with the other actors or even if you are the right height, weight, or skin color to fill the overall look of the production. You cannot change any of this, so why not just enjoy the callback?

In addition to logging the details of each audition for future referencing, the audition log also serves as a *journal* for you to jot down your impressions of the audition. *You are required to journal immediately after each audition.* I recommend that you find yourself a cheap coffee shop or a park bench or sidewalk corner, any place that is relatively quiet so that you can begin to record a stream-of-consciousness account regarding your experiences in the audition room. Write about how you felt, what you discovered, what you did really well, and what you would like to improve in the future. Please do not censor yourself; when it comes to your journal, these are your private thoughts—you are never wrong. They are just a pouring-out of feelings and emotions that will help you to gain perspective. Ugly thoughts and negative feelings are allowed and encouraged. Once the feelings are put into words and down on paper, you will feel a lightness that will help you to see things more clearly, thereby helping you to continue bringing your best to each and every future audition.

The reason that I insist on journaling is this: What do you think happens to an actress who does not journal following her audition? Unfortunately, what takes place is that the actress begins to carry around negative feelings from each previous audition experience; her "what ifs" are not resolved, and the negativity becomes a part of her overall audition package. I am sure that we have all spotted those performers who are carrying the weight of the world on their shoulders. They are what we call jaded, and although often extremely talented, they don't get very far.

We all know that the act of auditioning—of putting ourselves on the line to be judged by strangers, over and over, often without feedback—is a very unnatural process that can be emotionally debilitating. Because actors often have a difficult time separating themselves from their work, they carry every negative experience

Items That Belong in Your "Go Bag"

- Music rep book
- Headshots and resumes
- Dance shoes (for dance calls)
- Small towel
- Hair and makeup products (again, for dance calls; men should carry pressed translucent powder to diminish the shine)
- Thank-you cards (already stamped)
- Pen
- Pencil with sharpener
- Highlighter
- Small stapler (optional)
- Tape recorder (with spare batteries) or phone with recorder
- Audition log
- Journal
- Aspirin, throat lozenges, hair ties, snack, and bottled water

into their next audition or, worse, into their personal lives. For this reason, I insist that my clients spend at least ten minutes jotting down their feelings about each audition experience as a way of getting it out of their heads and onto the paper. This allows them to free up space—mental and emotional—so that they are freely and fully available for the next audition. The next time you are at a casting call, take a look around at the faces of the other performers and notice who seems to be open and emotionally available and who just looks beat up by the business. This is a tough business; don't let it beat you up—journal!

THE ACTOR'S FINANCES

This is the part of the actor's industry that excites most working professionals. The knowledge that an actor is able to write off a great many of their expenses—from headshots to dance shoes, hair products, even movie tickets—seems to make becoming an independent contractor worthwhile! Thankfully, the U.S. government understands that, for a performing artist, finding work is a full-time job; therefore, almost everything that costs money to reach that goal is considered a tax deduction.

The following are some suggestions on tax-deductible items for which you want to keep receipts. Out of respect for accountants and the work that they do, I only give you a small sampling:

- Stage makeup
- Haircuts for shows
- Hair products (used for shows only)
- Mileage to and from auditions and shows
- Tickets to productions (including movies and movie rentals)
- Promotional tickets (for agents, casting directors, etc., to come see your work)
- Telephone used for business purposes
- Business equipment and office supplies
- Website (and other marketing materials)
- Headshots and resumes

- Other industry-related photos
- Equity membership dues (and other union dues)
- Subscriptions (*Backstage* online, other newspapers and magazines)

The list goes on!

There are, however, some things that people think are write-offs that are not. Bathing suits and other clothing items are not write-offs (unless you are a swimsuit model). Everyday makeup does not count either. Over-the-counter medication cannot be written off, although prescription medications can be. There is a large list of dos and don'ts when it comes to filing receipts and taxes. It is best to go over every one of these with your accountant because every dollar adds up.

There are many parts to managing your finances, not the least of which includes working with a budget and filing your taxes. Again, I strongly urge you to add an accountant to your growing number of team members. A knowledgeable accountant will help you figure out which budgeting system is best for someone with your financial literacy and emotional disposition (finances are like food, and many of us have an emotional connection to each). The accountant will also assist you in creating a strategy for filing your receipts and then itemizing each category for maximum claim. You can also incorporate if you decide to do so later in your career. The benefit to incorporating yourself is that you separate the personal you from the business you. This is especially important as your career grows and you want to protect your personal assets (e.g., your home and personal bank accounts) from negative business matters that you might face throughout your career.

Similar to acquiring an agent, the best way to find a reputable accountant is to ask your peers for references. Someone whose career is doing slightly better than yours is the perfect person to ask; the accountant might just be pivotal in helping you to transition to the next level of your career. I have been with my accountant, Ruth Beltran, for many years (and many life experiences). Not only has Ruth been a resource for all things financial and business, but she also has been an informed guide in such processes as incorporating myself, as well as purchasing a home. She has been invaluable to me in helping me to see my dreams in detail and take practical steps toward fulfilling these.

At first, hiring an accountant may seem like an added expense; however, having an accountant is much like signing with an agent: You may not *need* them to get work, but as you continue to build your brand and work consistently, you will be grateful to have someone to help you keep your finances straight. The accountant is the professional who will help you to claim your rightful deductions, thereby getting you the greatest tax refund allowable so that you can focus your real attention on your career as a working professional.

Now that you have the tools, organizing your home office should be a breeze. Pick up the essentials to set up your space, work on filling your "go bag," and begin to master the basics of finance. You are the CEO of You, Incorporated, and it's time to start earning a living doing what you've trained to do!

Success Strategy 16

────────○────────

Finance Your
Developing Career

LISA GOLD, CEO OF Act Outside the Box, posits that the failure to finance one's career is the number-one reason 97 percent of the 60,000 theatre and musical theatre college graduates wind up leaving the industry before the end of their third year as a working professional. Without this, you are stuck in what most performers call the catch-22 of becoming a working professional: "I need to fund my career, but I first need the job in order to be able to afford to fund my career." Success strategy 16 is designed to propel your career to the next level by suggesting ways to help you finance each of the previous strategies discussed in this handbook.

> A major key to success lies in your ability to organize your finances at the start of your career.

Unless you have endless financial support from either a trust fund or super-supportive parents, financing your career most often entails acquiring a survival or parallel job (we discuss the differences later in this chapter) that keeps you employed during your first three years as a working professional. Even those who find performance work early on must still understand that it takes about three years of planting seeds in this industry before their efforts begin to produce consistent results. The necessary things in life—

eating a healthy meal, paying rent, buying a subway card or gas for your car to get to auditions and work—all demand a somewhat reliable paycheck. And then there is the challenge of funding the less urgent yet still important production costs of taking and reproducing new headshots, updating websites, paying union dues, and the like. All of these are part of the working professional's to-do list; yet without the ability to finance your career, you will likely crash and burn and be forced to resort to the dreaded backup plan that your parents always insisted you have. As an antidote to this, you must set yourself up with a flexible job that supports your performance career while also helping you to pay for the bare necessities. This is where the survival or parallel job comes in!

SURVIVAL OR PARALLEL JOBS: LAND A JOB THAT SUPPORTS YOUR CAREER

For those professionals who have already been pounding the pavement, I am sure that you have begun to feel the catch-22 of needing experience to get work yet needing work to get experience. This is frustrating, almost debilitating; however, it is extremely common in many professions, not just ours. As discussed in success strategy 12, "Get 'Them' to Trust You," volunteering is a very good way to gain experience and to increase your resume credits while also establishing industry connections. Although you should notice drastic changes in your career once you begin to implement these success strategies, I still caution that it takes approximately three years before you begin to see *consistent* results. To me, the most important thing that you need in order to survive these first three years is a job that supports your career. This job is referred to in our industry as the *survival job*.

The Survival Job

The term *survival job* is used to refer to *any type of work that would cover the basic costs of living, the bare minimum needed to survive*. In fact, as I was researching *survival job*, the very first thing that popped up in the taskbar, even before I was finished typing, was "survival jobs *for actors*." This suggests that we actors are the usual suspects who are seeking this type of employment.

However, times have changed, and survival jobs are not only jobs that pay you a minimum wage in order to eat and pay your rent. Today's actors need much more than the basics; you need to earn enough to pay for travel (subway, gas, etc.), cleaning audition clothing, classes (voice lessons, acting studio, dance classes), website management, and other career-related needs. Some survival jobs work better than others because they provide flexibility with scheduling. Others still provide the ability for greater income. Some survival jobs can even give you a sense of stability. To help inspire your imagination, I have put together a detailed and comparative list of survival jobs for you to use as a springboard in creating your own sideline work (see table 16.1).

Table 16.1. Comprehensive List of Survival and Parallel Jobs

Waiter	Web Designer	Exotic Dancer
Bartender	Voice-Over Artist	Model
Tutor	Teaching Artist	Spokesperson
Voice Teacher	Adjunct Professor	Casting Assistant
Vocal Coach	Nanny	Lighting Assistant
Monologue Coach	Dog Walker	Costume Assistant
Bookkeeper	Telemarketer	Prop Master
Housekeeper	Phone Operator	Laundromat Worker
Proofreader	Retail Associate	Dry Cleaning Assistant
Caterer	Sales Associate	Receptionist
Wardrobe Assistant	Literary Manager	Temp Worker
Nutritionist	Box Office Assistant/	Typist
Fitness Instructor	Administration	Food Services
Martial Arts Instructor	Theatre Usher	Massage Therapist
Translator	Transportation Driver	Real Estate Agent
	(Bus, Taxi, Uber)	

The Parallel Job

In contrast to the survival job, there is another type of employment that I recommend for your consideration. This is called the *parallel job*. The term *parallel job* was coined by Patricia "Patch"

Schwadron, career counselor supervisor at the Career Center, formerly the Actors Fund Work Program, in New York City and longtime friend of mine. She defines *parallel job* as a "job that you enjoy *as much as*, or *almost as much as*, your work as an actor or performer. It is employment that you love doing as much as you enjoy being in the performing arts."

Some of the most fun parallel jobs that I've heard of include working as a nanny (for those who love working with children), being a web designer (excellent for creative, computer-savvy types), running a home-cleaning service (flexible hours), working as a delivery person (for those who hate office work and prefer the great outdoors), and teaching piano or voice or some other skill. The parallel job is in direct contrast to the survival job, which can often deplete you of your joy and actually challenge your performance career. Such survival jobs as waiting tables (a great way to make money yet horrible for the voice), bartending (late nights = rough mornings), and real estate agent (great payout but very unreliable) can be financially rewarding but very often take a toll on the actor's instrument (voice, body, mind, and emotions). Considering that one person's survival job may be another's parallel employment, I decided not to separate the list, and I also use the terms interchangeably. For fun, try comparing your list of parallel jobs with that of a friend to see how different your choices are!

Six Pitfalls of Survival or Parallel Jobs

The following are six areas of caution to keep in mind as you select your sideline work!

Staying Up Late

Most auditions occur in the morning (9 a.m. sign up with a 10 a.m. start time). What this means is that most performers have to show up at 8 a.m., 7 a.m., 6 a.m., or earlier. This can become quite challenging when you are up until 2 a.m. tending bar or working your catering job. Add to this your commuting time as well as the time that it takes you to decompress and fall asleep, and you have the perfect storm for skipping that audition.

This is where planning and organization are keys to succeeding. You have to be extremely organized (which you are if you have been working the success strategies) and able to set up your audition package (rep book, audition clothes, "go bag," etc.) ahead of time. Sometimes you need to do this an entire day in advance in order to avoid the urge to skip going to the audition.

In all honesty, I have no words of wisdom here. It is extremely difficult. I know this very well, for I was there for many, many years (and return every few years). All I can say is that showing up is about 80 percent of booking the job. Survival jobs can be a major challenge to showing up; it is so very difficult to show up when you are tired as heck from the night before. It doesn't matter—set two alarms and get yourself to the audition. No excuses. This is what the industry lovingly refers to as "paying your dues." We all have to do it, so no excuses—show up!

Damaging Your Voice

Another byproduct of being up late with your survival or parallel job is that you start getting sick or are too tired to speak or sing with technique. This, again, is a challenge that you have to work on by getting your rest when you can, as well as by taking your vitamins with consistency. Always get your own doctor's advice tailored to your health needs and history, but it is common practice for performers to take over-the-counter products that help boost their health and immunity. This list may include a daily antioxidant, vitamin B, and vitamin D, and have your reserve of vitamin C, zinc lozenges, Fisherman's Friend throat lozenges, and Airborne ready for when you are feeling a bit overextended. You are going to get sick from time to time; this is when technique kicks in.

Unless you are so sick that you will show yourself in a really, really bad light, you should always show up. Auditors can tell if you are sick, and if they see that you might be what they are looking for, they will call you back in order to give you a second chance in the hopes of seeing you at your best. This happens all the time, but it *never* happens to those who don't show up.

Being "Typed" by Industry Professionals

I remember accepting a cater-waitering job at an event that many industry professionals were attending. I thought, "Great! I'll get to meet professionals and listen to their conversations, maybe network a bit." Well, this was far from the case; in fact, it quickly became apparent to me that being in this environment with a white shirt, black vest, and tray in my hands might just be detrimental to my career. I finished out the night but was careful to ask about the clientele in future catering gigs.

Although actors are expected to work such jobs as waiting tables at restaurants or bartending at high-end bars, these are public areas where people come and go. Catering someone's private event is somehow different; the guests usually know each other and are there for more than a brief dinner or drink. The conversations are longer and more intimate, and the impressions tend to last longer. Being a server in such an environment can be like go-go dancing at a high-end bar: The money's good, but if you're seen by the wrong people, it can really color their impression of you as an artist. Of course, some performers have been able to turn these encounters into next steps in their careers, especially those with USPs like *domestic* and *helper,* or *provocative* and *seductive.* It's really just a matter of personal choice and comfort level, but you have to make a conscious decision about this. In this industry, you are always "on."

Risk of Other Types of Injury

There are jobs that are so physically demanding that you may wish to avoid these if they threaten your physical well-being. Work as a mechanic might be iffy; a furniture mover may also risk back injuries. Stocking shelves can be a good gig, but it depends on the weight that you are constantly lifting.

There are also some jobs within the performing arts of which I would really caution you to be wary. "Industrials" are great-paying, short-term gigs in the performing arts. Because of the compressed rehearsal periods and lightning speed yet chaotic day of event, performers (dancers, tumblers, and aerialists) can often suffer injuries. Plus, the fact that this is typically noninsured work, you really have to be responsible for your own well-being when performing in industrials. I had a very good friend who was dancing for the Super Bowl and was lifted high in the air only to have his harness break. He plunged forty feet to the ground and broke his hip and has never been the same. Fortunately, the producing company was a large enterprise, so at least his medical insurance bills were covered, as well as some pain and suffering. Yet I do not believe that you can put a price tag on a broken hip and ruined dance career.

If you land this type of work, then make certain that you are covered by their insurance policy if possible or have your own coverage. Most especially, make sure that you give yourself a good warm-up, and do not push yourself beyond your healthy limit. Once you have the job, it is very rare that they will fire you from an industrial; therefore, do not be afraid to protect yourself and make the job work for you.

Takes You Out of Town

Anyone in a big city knows that one of the worst things that you can do when you are building your network of professionals is to suddenly pick up and leave town. This means that not only will you be unavailable to audition and possibly accept work but also that you will really upset those who are now trying to get you seen for the work. Accepting a survival job that takes you out of town is extremely detrimental to establishing your career in the local theatre community. If you are "out of sight, out of mind," then this often means that you may be forced to start back at square one for establishing yourself.

Of course, this is different from acting jobs; in the early stages of your career as a working professional, you should welcome performance work in regional theatres, on cruise ships, in international work, whatever it takes to build your resume. It is also often in your best interest to accept a production contract on a national tour if booked; this obviously helps you to continue building your reputation as a trustworthy professional.

The challenges are intense for actors of television, film, commercials, and stage work who want to solidify their reputations in a major city's market; this often means turning down work that takes them out of town. Some examples of the larger and well-known theatre communities are the Steppenwolf and Goodman Theatres in Chicago, the Ahmanson Theatre in Los Angeles, the Alliance in Atlanta, and, of course, the Broadway community in New York City. This is especially true once you are signed with an agent, as they often prefer that you stay put so that they can submit you for local work. The only time that going away is seen to be favorable for an agency is when the agent is making money off of you on a major contract. If you are trying to build your network and reputation within a certain city's market, then stay put!

Inordinate Amount of Stress

Some people find themselves caring a little too much about their nontheatre survival jobs, especially if the work deals with young people (e.g., nanny, tutor, coach). Occasionally, they become so emotionally involved that they are unable to focus on their performing career because they are emotionally drained by the day job.

This is where journaling becomes essential, as well as being able to speak with a trained professional (your own coach or therapist) to help devise strategies for remaining compassionate without becoming empathetic and taking on the survival job's struggles and challenges. I admit that this has been a challenge for me when coaching my clients. Although I have experienced enough to trust that they are getting closer to their dreams and goals, watching them struggle through their own individual journeys is tough for me. But as they say, *"Lo que no mata engorda"* ("What doesn't kill you makes you stronger"; well, really, it says, "What doesn't kill you makes you *fatter*"—in Puerto Rico, everything is about food). But I digress.

It's essential that you do the occasional check-in session with your coach (or even best friend) to make sure that you are focusing on important things like your acting career. Anything that pulls you away from this, even if for humanitarian reasons, must be kept in check; otherwise, you will find yourself doing more as a volunteer for the arts than actually earning a living in the profession. As the late actor and choreographer (and my good friend) Tim Albrech used to say, "If you are not making a living in theatre, it isn't a profession—*it's a hobby!*"

Which Survival or Parallel Jobs Would Be Best for Me?

How do you decide which survival job might be suitable for you, or better yet, which parallel job would be worth exploring and investing in?

Do you consider yourself to:

- Be a morning person?
- Like being around people?
- Enjoy hanging out with large groups?
- Prefer to work alone?
- Work well with your hands?
- Prefer detail-oriented work?

Now is the time to figure out your first—or next—survival or parallel job. Remember to take into consideration where you live and what opportunities are available. Also consider how much money you need to make to stay afloat. Go back and journal using the sidebar questions from this chapter. Last, choose three jobs from the comprehensive list of survival and parallel jobs in table 16.1 that you would consider exploring or researching for your next gig. There are also many online resources that can help you to separate all work into such categories as service, advising, artistic, clerical, recreational, analytical, or mechanical. Consider which of these categories you prefer, and use this to help you create your top three survival and parallel jobs. And, as always, feel free to come up with your own possibilities. After all, you know yourself better than anyone else does!

---○---

Negotiate a
Profitable Contract

MANY EARLY-CAREER PROFESSIONALS start to feel guilty when even *thinking* about negotiating. They feel that they will be tagged with words like *greedy* or *demanding* when attempting to improve the terms of a performance contract. Of course, if you can afford it, then it is entirely acceptable to hire an agent, lawyer, or other legal representative to negotiate on the your behalf. But most of the time, the young actor or the transitioning professional is charged with the task of negotiating his or her own contracts.

Consequently, it is essential for young professionals to develop some strategies for managing this aspect of their careers. There is nothing more deflating than showing up to a theatre gig and finding out that everyone is making more money for the same job or that someone has negotiated their own bedroom while others are sharing three to a room or that another actor was reimbursed for her travel while you had to provide your own way to the theatre.

In his top ten tips for negotiating a contract, author and attorney Mark Anderson suggests that we give ourselves time and space to negotiate. Along these lines, I insist that actors give themselves at least twenty-four hours before accepting a job offer. This is often very challenging for a young actor who is so excited to get that highly anticipated telephone call. They blurt out, "I'll take it!" even before the entire offer has been outlined.

The problem with accepting an offer "as is" is that, in the performing arts, *it is your job to negotiate.* This may be true for any career, but it is especially true in ours, given that only 22 percent of all professional (AEA) actors are working at any given time. For this reason, actors are often seen as being desperate for work. Yet the *professional, working actor* understands that negotiating a contract is just as much a part of their job as memorizing lines or showing up to rehearsals on time. If the parameters of the position are not clearly outlined and satisfactory at the very beginning of the contract, then the actor will not be at his or her best. This affects the quality of the actor's work as well as the overall production. As you can see, then, it is in everyone's interest that the expectations be clarified from the very start.

Negotiating a Contract: Step 1

The following is an example of how an actor might go about beginning the negotiation process:

Thank you so much for the offer. I am so excited for this opportunity. From what I can tell, everything looks great, and I will need a couple of days to look over the specifics to make sure I don't have any questions. Can I get back to you first thing Monday morning?

Negotiating a Contract: Step 2

This is part 2 of the negotiation (in this case, the Monday morning telephone call):

Thank you again for this amazing offer. I am thrilled to begin working with you. I have a couple of questions that I hope you can help me with. In order to do my best job for the production, I would like to request . . .

Breaking Down the Steps
to Negotiating a Contract

I want to remind you that I am neither a lawyer nor a contract specialist. My suggestions are coming to you solely as an audition coach and career consultant who has helped countless actors and performers through this sometimes very uncomfortable part of the process.

I once coached a client who, after many months of auditioning, finally booked a dream contract on a ship. Having served two back-to-back six-month contracts performing on a ship, I had an idea of what might be important to someone embarking on this type of project. Together we outlined strategies that included her own room on the ship as well as several hundred dollars more than what she had been originally offered. My client was very uncomfortable asking for more money; in the end, she trusted me, and because of this, she became one of the highest paid performers on this ship! Although you *never* want to discuss money with your coworkers, this experience taught her (and reminded me) that it is our job to ask for what you need in order to do your best work for the producers. She also had to clearly outline what her nonnegotiables were (in this case, she *needed* her own room) and what was the least that she would accept (remember that she was willing to do it for the original offer). In the end, she was able to make a huge dent in her student loan while entertaining audiences *and traveling the world!*

The following is a simple, six-step formula for negotiating your own contract.

Step 1: Express Enthusiasm

A genuine exclamation of excitement is appropriate and necessary to let the casting director know that you are in. For some casting directors, calling the actor with an offer is often the best part of their job, so let them hear your enthusiasm.

Step 2: Be Grateful

"Thank you so much for the offer" is usually all it takes to reaffirm to the person on the other end that they have made the right decision.

Step 3: Ask for Time to Look over the Details

As stated previously, never, ever say "yes" to an offer without giving yourself at least twenty-four hours to consider the impact that it will have on your life or to come up with a list of negotiation terms. You need to read over the fine print (or, better yet, have your friend's uncle who is an attorney do it for you). The producers understand that, once you sign, you must abide by every detail of the contract; therefore, they almost always honor the intelligent actor who requests a bit of time to read over the details. Sometimes they will give you a deadline: "We need it by this Thursday at 3 p.m." Occasionally, they will warn you that they need an answer the following morning or they will offer the job to the next person in their queue. Say, "Thanks, will do!" and then start reading and working on your negotiation terms.

Step 4: Create Your List of Needs versus Wants

Once you have read through and understood the contract, first make a list of what you will *need* in order to say yes to the contract (also known as your nonnegotiables). Then follow this with a list of *what you would like to have* in order to make your life better. A "need" might include a livable wage, your own room or a solo seat on the bus (this is often a deal-breaker for those on a national bus-and-truck tour), hair supplies to maintain your show hair, or even a "four-week out" if you have been in final callbacks for a Broadway show (we discuss this one later in the chapter). A "want" may include tickets to the show for your family, an understudy credit, or round-trip transportation to and from the theatrical venue. Needs and wants are very individual for each actor; again, you must be clear in what you would like and what you will simply not do without.

Step 5: Write Out Your Response

Make sure that you have written out your contract terms prior to calling the company manager back. It must sound as if you are simply having a discussion, yet having everything written down keeps you from being overcome with nerves or getting thrown off of your game by the negotiator's responses. Do rehearse this (i.e., perform a mock negotiation run) prior to making the actual phone call. If you are negotiating via e-mail, then simply make certain that your e-mail is brief yet clearly outlines your negotiation terms.

Step 6: Perform a Mock Negotiation

As with most of our strategies, I highly recommend that you and a friend run through the telephone call as if it is the actual negotiation. Ask your friend to play hardball; the tougher they are with you, the more prepared you will be in the actual negotiation conversation. Remember, all you are doing is outlining your needs and wants and then either accepting or declining the offer. It's that simple—and it's your job!

> *Always get everything in writing.* If the negotiated terms do not appear in the contract, then insist that a rider (an addendum to the contract) be drafted, signed, and remitted to you. If it is not in writing, then *it does not exist!*

In the actual negotiation discussion, remember to do the following:

1. Express gratitude and enthusiasm—again, remind them of how grateful and excited you are at the opportunity of joining them for this project.
2. Mention that you are completely onboard with the project and just have a couple of questions—you are *practically* saying yes without actually committing to the contract until everything has been spelled out. Say something along the lines of "I am onboard with the project, and I have a couple of questions." Notice that I said *and* and not *but*. By choosing the more positive connector, you are moving forward with the project; if you use the negative *but*, this indicates to them that you are not yet sure if you want to accept the gig—this is not something they want to hear. Remem-

ber success strategy 8, "Conquer Audition Nerves"? You must turn every negative into a positive, and this is another chance in which doing so is essential.

3. State your negotiation term(s) in the form of a question—stating your terms as questions (e.g., "Are there opportunities to eat in the dining room with the staff?") helps the company manager to maintain control and does not put them on the defensive. "I need extra money for food" or "I want to eat in the dining hall with the others" sounds like a demand; unless you carry star power, this will often not work out in your favor.

4. Reference the theatre's integrity—when I coach a client, I usually state the questions like, "It would be extremely helpful to have my own seat on the bus so that I am rested and ready to do my best work for the theatre. Is this an option?" Notice how you have made the seat not about your own comfort level but about the show—their show! Another example is "Are there opportunities to eat at least one meal at the theatre? As someone still paying off student loans, this would make a huge difference in my mental state and allow me to be completely focused on the job and needs of the show." Even if the answer to this question is a "no," the company manager will almost always look for ways to provide some sort of meal assistance (a shared kitchen or an offer to provide a list of cheap area restaurants). The goal here is to get them on your side by showing that your needs are all about *their* theatre or film shoot or commercial.

5. Be prepared to accept or decline immediately—once your questions have been asked, be ready to look at your list and either accept or decline the offer. But be warned, producers are not really used to actors declining an offer. I recall being blacklisted in New York City by a major casting director who was so upset with me for declining to attend a callback that she left me a scathing voice mail. It upset me so much because I thought, "How many rejections have I received from you?" Now I'm not proposing that you turn down a job after accepting it. Just remember that the only power that an actor has is to say "no" to that offer. Once the offer is accepted, the terms are on paper, and you are bound by the contract. Therefore, if after

your negotiations you do not feel that you are able to abide by the conditions, then simply express your gratitude and gracefully walk away. Do not argue, do not try to renegotiate; just say "thank you" and move on to the next audition.

ITEMS FOR NEGOTIATION

- *Salary*—Whenever possible, ask for an amount greater than you want, and be willing to settle for somewhere in the middle.
- *Per Diem*—This is monetary compensation separate from the actor's salary, usually for the provision of food or lodging when on tour.
- *Bonus and Signing Bonus*—This is important if they say that there is no way to negotiate a higher salary. Oftentimes, actors can negotiate payment in the form of a nice stipend if they complete the run of the show or can sometimes negotiate a lump sum at the start of the contract just for saying "yes."
- *Room and Board*—One of the most commonly negotiated terms, actors can often negotiate lodging and meals, especially when performing out of their state of residence. Lodging may be a shared room with another actor, a room in someone's home, or even one's own room in a hotel or motel. Meals may range from use of a kitchen, actual cooked meals in a restaurant, a continental breakfast, and so on.
- *Travel to and from the Theatre*—Do not be afraid to request air travel when possible, and more important, insist on receiving your return ticket at the start of the contract. You may also request times of day that are best for you to travel or reimbursement for money spent on travel if preferred.
- *Conflicts*—It is important to ask for the two days off that you need to attend your brother's wedding as part of the contract negotiation discussion; otherwise, you will probably miss the most important day of his life!
- *Dressing Rooms and Miscellaneous Backstage*—There are some instances in which you may wish to ask for your own dressing room or a shared room with no more than one or two actors, a dressing room with a bathroom and shower in it, and various

other backstage needs (e.g., access to purified water, specialty drinks, availability of snacks).

- *Rooming Assignment*—If touring, you can request to room with a specific person in the cast or, as in my case, to *not* live with another cast member (I prefer to live with a stage manager or member of the crew).
- *First Right of Refusal*—If you are performing an early incarnation of a new work, you may wish to request the first right to refuse the role should the project move forward. Otherwise, you will do the early work without the guarantee that you will continue with the project if it becomes hugely successful. This term is most popular when performing in a workshop production or pilot that has the possibility of going into full production but that may leave the actor out of the running should the producers decide to bring on another actor (oftentimes a well-known, bigger box-office draw). The actor must be bought out of their contract should this occur.
- *Four-Week Out*—Much like a housing rental agreement in which you give thirty days' notice to vacate the premises, the four-week out means that you must give the theatre notice four weeks prior to "vacating" your role. The number of weeks can vary from two weeks to several months. The value here is in being able to end a contract during the actual run of the show for such reasons as other work, personal well-being, or almost any other reason. This is most helpful for up-and-coming talent who expect to receive another, more lucrative contract and gives the producers sufficient time to hire and rehearse the replacement actor.
- *Understudy or Cover*—For early performers, I insist that they negotiate an additional duty as an understudy (i.e., the right to *cover* another larger role) whenever possible as a way of continuing to build their resume. Unless it is an Equity contract, this usually does not cost the producers any additional money yet provides them with added protection. If you are hired as a chorus performer or an extra on a film, offering to cover another larger role (lead, featured extra) makes you more valuable to the producers. In other words, it is a win-win situation, so do this!
- *Tickets to Performance*—You may negotiate comps (complimentary tickets) for your visiting family, friends, and even industry folks.

- *Billing*—This can make a difference for someone playing a larger role in an ensemble piece. Usually, the higher up your name is on the show program, the more notice you receive. Billing can be a great negotiating term for performers transitioning to larger roles.
- *Shoes*—If you are performing in a new production, you may ask to have your shoes provided or even to keep the footwear upon completion of the contact.
- *Hair and Makeup*—For some, maintenance of hair and makeup can often run into the hundreds per month, so negotiating specific needs into the contract is a standard process.
- *Personal Assistant*—Self-explanatory.
- *Copy or Reel*—Always request a copy of the film in which you are performing or of the show if the theatre is filming, so that you can add clips to your professional online reel.

Shaun Nerney

Web: www.shaunnerney.com
E-mail: lmnop@qmail.com
Cell: 555-123-4567

Dear Katie,

I wanted to start off by saying I am thrilled with the possibility of working for RWS. After looking over your email, I just have a couple of questions. I was wondering if it would be possible for me to arrive on-site May 15? My date of availability on my UPTA sheet when I originally filled it out online my date was around that time. I believe I could make the 12th work but the 15th of May would be ideal. I was also wondering the possibility of having my own room? I know the amount of work a swing holds on their shoulders and to have my own private space will be conducive and reflect the quality of work I feel that RWS deserves from me. My next question is about a per diem for food? If that is not an option, are there any discounts for workers of Kennywood in the area? The final question I have is that I was wondering if it were possible to request the first right of refusal for the first role that becomes available? I would love to hop right in and assume the role. I know that I am meant to be on stage and would love that opportunity. Thank you so much!

Best,

Shaun Nerney

Sample negotiation. *Courtesy of Shaun Nerney.*

OTHER INDUSTRY TERMS RELATED
TO CONTRACT NEGOTIATIONS

- *Favored Nations*—If the producer says that the contract is a Favored Nations contract, then this means that everyone in the company is receiving the same salary. But do not fear: You can always get around this by negotiating a signing bonus, per diem, your own room, and any of the other items discussed previously.
- *Rider*—This is an addendum to the contract. If the producer insists that you sign by the deadline, then they can always add an additional attachment to the original contract; this addition is called a rider.
- *Release (of Rights to Images, Likeness, Etc.)*—if you are ever asked to sign a release, understand the terms of the contract, as you are signing over your rights to all photos, images, and so on for use by the theatre. This is most common in commercial print work. If the release states that it is "in perpetuity," this means that they can make money off your photo forever. However, most releases have an end date (e.g., one year, two years).

Bonus

Included are some current minimum salaries for various kinds of industry jobs that might be helpful for you to know prior to beginning your negotiations. Salaries are current at the time of publication.

- Film extra: $50–150/day
- Stand-in: $100–250/day
- Day player on a feature film: $759/day
- Costarring role on television sitcom: $2,700
- Theme park: $150/day
- Convention work: $150–250/day ($225–300/day if you demonstrate product)
- Voice-over: $125 for first hour, $75 each additional hour (more for national or regional spots)
- Commercials: $627.75/day + additional pay every thirteen-week cycle (variable amounts depending on many factors, including fifteen- or thirty-second time slots, regional/national/international, and others)
- Commercial print: $200/hour
- Stunts: $300/day for nonunion; $596/day for union
- Product narration: $400/day
- Off-Broadway theatre: $566–1,008/week
- Production contract (Broadway): $1,861/week

Epilogue

CONGRATULATIONS! You've integrated the seventeen success strategies for becoming a professional actor into your business, You, Incorporated. When you first picked up this book, you demonstrated your commitment to turning your dreams into reality. Instead of just dreaming about a career in the performing arts, you took action and are beginning to see steady results. With *The Professional Actor's Handbook: From Casting Call to Curtain Call*, you are literally mapping out your route as a working professional.

The key to every success is combining the knowledge you need (check) with daily actions (check) and, perhaps most important, an unstoppable tenacity to accomplish your goals (check). By applying these strategies, you have proven that you are in the percentage of those who actually "make it" into the league of the *working professionals*. A working professional never stops working, evolving, reinventing him- or herself, so keep taking action and keep your commitments to yourself. From one working professional to another, I encourage you to stay in touch by visiting our website at www.julioagustin.com, where you can sign up for our monthly motivational and celebratory newsletter, book a personal coaching session, or receive news on the latest in the Transition Workshop Studio. You can also interact with each other via our social media connections to remain informed of the most up-to-date industry news, opportunities, free workshops, links to useful resources, and much more.

Remember that sharing both your struggles and successes is part of helping others making their way through the industry, so please do share your news. I promise that even the worst audition experience will eventually become a funny story—well, if not for you, for someone else! Remember: *Lo que no mata engorda.*

Resources

ACTING COACHES

Cronican, Erin (business consultant). http://theactorsenterprise.org
Galligan-Stierle, Aaron (audition coach). http://www.aarongs.com
Gold, Lisa (business consultant). http://www.actoutsidethebox.com
Miko, Casey (material consultant). http://caseymiko.wixsite.com/casey
miko/consultation

ACTING TECHNIQUES

Adler, Stella. *The Technique of Acting* (Bantam, 1990).
Benedetti, Robert, and Cicely Berry. *The Actor at Work* (Prentice-Hall, 2008).
Caine, Michael. *Acting in Film* (Applause, 1997).
Haase, Cathy. *Acting for Film* (Allworth Press, 2003).
Moore, Tracey, and Allison Bergman. *Acting the Song: Performance Skills for the Musical Theatre* (Skyhorse, 2008).

AUDITIONING

Bishop, Nancy. *Secrets from the Casting Couch* (Bloomsbury, 2009).
Cohen, Daren, and Michael Perilstein. *Complete Professional Audition* (Back Stage Books, 2005).

Craig, David. *On Singing on Stage*, new rev. ed. (Applause, 1990).

Flom, Jonathan. *Get the Callback: The Art of Auditioning for Musical Theatre*, 2nd ed. (Rowman and Littlefield, 2016).

Hunt, Gordon. *How to Audition—for TV, Movies, Commercials, Plays and Musicals* (Harper Resource, 2002).

Kayes, Gilyanne, and Jeremy Fisher. *Successful Singing Auditions* (Routledge, 2002).

Sanders, Sheri. *Rock the Audition* (Hal Leonard Books, 2011).

THE BUSINESS OF ACTING

Beardsley, Elaine Keller. *Working in Commercials* (Focal Press, 1993).

Cohen, Robert. *Acting Professionally* (Palgrave MacMillan, 2009).

Donahue, Tim, and Jim Patterson. *Theater Careers: A Realistic Guide* (University of South Carolina Press, 2012).

Flom, Jonathan. *Act Like It's Your Business: Branding and Marketing Strategies for Actors* (Scarecrow Press, 2013).

Henry, Mari Lyn, and Lynne Rogers. *How to Be a Working Actor* (Back Stage Books, 2008).

Hubbard, Valorie, and Lea Tolub Brandenburg. *The Actor's Workbook: How to Become a Working Actor* (Pearson, 2008).

Menninger, Carl, and Lori Hammel. *Minding the Edge* (Waveland Press, 2012).

O'Neil, Brian. *Acting as a Business* (Heinemann, 2014).

Travers, Dallas. *The Tao of Business* (Love Your Life, 2008).

COSTUMES

Lewandowski, Elizabeth. *The Complete Costume Dictionary* (Scarecrow Press, 2012).

DANCE STUDIOS (LOS ANGELES)

Debbie Reynolds. http://drdancestudio.com

Edge. http://www.edgepac.com

Millennium Dance Complex. http://millenniumdancecomplex.com

DANCE STUDIOS (NEW YORK CITY)

Alvin Ailey. https://www.alvinailey.org
Broadway Dance Center. https://www.broadwaydancecenter.com
Peridance. http://www.peridance.com
Steps. https://www.stepsnyc.com

HEADSHOT PHOTOGRAPHERS

Hurley, Peter. https://peterhurley.com
Loper, Joe. http://www.gphotony.com
Matter, Jordan. http://www.jordanmatter.com
Mosier, Jeffrey. http://jeffreymosierphotography.com
Offidani, Brian. http://www.brianoffidani.com/headshots
Treadway, Scott. http://www.scotttreadwayphotography.com
Weingart, Keven (Los Angeles). http://www.edgyheadshots.com

HEADSHOT REPRODUCTIONS

ABC Pictures. http://abcpictures.com
Overnight Prints. https://www.overnightprints.com
Postcards.com. http://www.postcards.com
Precision Photos. http://www.precisionphotos.com
Quick Color Custom Photo Lab. http://quickcolorlabnyc.com
Reproductions. http://reproductions.com
Vista Print. https://www.vistaprint.com

INTERNSHIPS, VOLUNTEERING, AND TRANSITIONAL WEBSITES

After College. https://www.aftercollege.com
Corporate Staffing. https://mustardlane.com
Idealist. http://www.idealist.org
Intern/Jobs. http://internjobs.com
Internships. http://www.tcg.org/artsearch
Merchandising Services. http://marqueemerchandise.com
Seat Fillers. http://www.play-by-play.com
Summer Internships. http://www.internweb.com
Volunteering Opportunities. http://www.volunteermatch.org

MAKEUP

Davis, Gretchen, and Mindy Hall. *The Makeup Artist Handbook: Techniques for Film, Television, Photography, and Theatre*, 2nd ed. (Focal Press, 2012).

MOVEMENT

Lust, Annette. *Bringing the Body to the Stage and Screen: Expressive Movement for Performers* (Scarecrow Press, 2012).

MUSICAL THEATRE

DeVenney, David P. *The New Broadway Song Companion* (Scarecrow Press, 2009).
Flom, Jonathan. *Get the Callback: The Art of Auditioning for Musical Theatre*, 2nd ed. (Rowman and Littlefield, 2016).
Hall, Karen. *So You Want to Sing Musical Theater* (Rowman and Littlefield, 2014).

RESOURCE ORGANIZATIONS AND PUBLICATIONS

The Actors Fund. http://actorsfund.org
Agent and Casting Directors Guides. http://www.nyactingagents.com/new-york-acting-business/acting-business-publications.html
Career Transition for Dancers. http://www.careertransition.org
The Holdon Log. http://www.holdonlog.com
The Season Overview. http://www.theseasonoverview.com

SITE RESOURCES

Actors Access. http://actorsaccess.com
The Actors Connection. http://www.actorsconnection.com

The Actors Greenroom. http://www.theactorsgreenroom.com
Answers for Dancers. www.answers4dancers.com
Backstage.com. http://www.backstage.com
The Call Sheet. http://www.backstage.com/resources
Casting Call. http://www.backstage.com/resources
Central Casting (background). http://www.centralcasting.com
L.A. Casting (background). http://www.lacasting.com
Now Casting (background). https://www.nowcasting.com
One-on-One (by audition). http://www.oneononenyc.com
Playbill.com. http://www.playbill.com/job/listing

STUDIOS

Atlantic Theatre Company. https://atlantictheater.org
Maggie Flanigan Studio. http://www.maggieflaniganstudio.com
Sande Shurin Studio. http://sandeshurin.com
Stella Adler Studio. http://www.stellaadler.com
T. Shreiber Studio. http://tschreiber.org
Tom Todoroff Studio. http://tomtodoroff.com
Upright Citizens Brigade. http://www.uprightcitizens.org

UNIONS

Actors' Equity Association (AEA). http://www.actorsequity.org
American Guild of Musical Artists (AGMA). http://www.musicalartists.org
American Guild of Variety Artists (AGVA). http://www.agvausa.com
Professional Dancers Society (PDS). http://www.professionaldancers
   society.org
Screen Actors Guild/American Federation of Television and Radio Artists
   (SAG-AFTRA). http://www.sagaftra.org

VOCAL COACHES (NEW YORK CITY)

Brunetti, David. http://www.actingsongs.com
Lavine, Michael. http://www.michaellavine.net
Miko, Casey. http://www.caseymiko.com

VOCAL SKILLS

Mabry, Sharon. *The Performing Life: A Singer's Guide to Survival* (Scarecrow Press, 2012).
One Voice: Integrating Singing and Theatre Voice Techniques (Waveland, 2012).

VOCAL TEACHERS (NEW YORK CITY)

Caplan, Liz. http://lizcaplan.com
Lifton, Deborah. http://deborahlifton.com
Semer, Neil. http://www.neilsemer.com
Wilkinson, Joleen. http://www.joleenwilkinson.com/about-2

WEBSITE HOSTING

Squarespace.com
Weebly.com
Wix.com

ADDITIONAL RESOURCES

Articles

Bennett, Drake. "Feeling Nervous? Don't Try to Calm Down—Get Excited," *Bloomberg*, December 31, 2013. http://www.bloomberg.com/news/articles/2013-12-31/feeling-nervous-dont-try-to-calm-down-get-excited.
Brooks, Alison Wood. "Get Excited: Reappraising Pre-Performance Anxiety as Excitement," *Journal of Experimental Psychology: American Psychological Association* 143, no. 3 (2014): 1144–58.
Smith, Jacquelyn. "How to Be a Great Mentor," *Forbes Magazine*, May 17, 2013.

Books

Beaudine, Bob. *The Power of Who: You Already Know Everyone You Need to Know* (Center Street, 2009).

Bolles, Richard N. *What Color Is Your Parachute?* (Ten Speed Press, 2016).
Heller, Joseph. *Catch-22* (Dell, 1968).
Homer and George Chapman. *The Odyssey* (Wordsworth Classics, 2002).
Pollak, Lindsey. *Getting from College to Career* (Harper, 2007).

Bookstores

The Drama Book Shop (New York City). http://www.dramabookshop.com
Samuel French Film and Theatre Bookshop (Hollywood). http://www
.samuelfrench.com/bookstore

Websites

Broadwayworld.com
Internet Broadway Database (IBDb)
Internet Movie Database (IMDb)
Playbillvault.com

Miscellaneous

Beltran, Ruth (industry accountant). Phone: (212) 213-0639
Gaudioso, Dr. Anthony. http://www.empowermentsource.com

Index

About the Authors

Julio Agustin (Julio A. Matos Jr.) has taught, directed, and performed on and off-Broadway, regionally, and internationally. His performing credits include featured roles in Broadway musicals (*Chicago* opposite Bebe Neuwirth, a revival of *Bells Are Ringing*, featured duet with Faith Prince); original companies of *Fosse*, *Women on the Verge of a Nervous Breakdown*, *Never Gonna Dance*, and *Steel Pier*; and the movies *Center Stage* and *The Producers*. He is also very active in commercials and commercial print.

He was most recently nominated for an Audelco Award for his work as director of the New Haarlem Arts Theatre's Latina-inspired production of *Sweet Charity*. He worked as the resident choreographer at the Hangar Theatre and is coconceiver of the musical *Out of Line* with composer John Franceschina, which was presented at Pennsylvania Centre Stage with a cast of Broadway veterans. He has directed and choreographed throughout the United States and is on the staff of the Mid-Atlantic Summer Dance Festival in Harrisonburg, Virginia.

In addition to coaching voice and acting, Julio teaches his monthly Transition Workshop Studio (www.JulioAgustin.com) to students, early-career professionals, and seasoned professionals seeking to reinvent themselves. He has taught master classes for the students of various dance and theatre training programs, including

Shenandoah Conservatory, Western Michigan University, Florida State University, the City College of New York, and others.

Julio received his bachelor of music degree from the Florida State University and his MFA in directing from Pennsylvania State University and is a member of the Society of Directors and Choreographers (SDC), Actor's Equity Association (AEA), Screen Actors Guild (SAG), American Federation of Television and Radio Artists (AFTRA), and the Voice and Speech Trainers Association (VASTA). He is an assistant professor of theatre and dance at James Madison University.

Kathleen Potts is an award-winning playwright, dramaturge, and academic. Recipient of the Eugene O'Neill Fellowship (O'Neill Playwrights' Conference, Waterbury, CT) and an aficionado of the new play process, her New York playwriting credits include *Miss Nowhere Diner*, winner of the Kennedy Center/American College Theatre Festival's Lorraine Hansberry Award and published by Dramatic Publishing Company; *F.H.O.D.O.M.*, a multimedia collaboration with Lydia Fort and Jeanette Oi-Suk Yew for the Women Center Stage Festival at the Culture Project; *Sexual Chemistry 911*, produced as part of the Manhattan Repertory Theatre's Summer One-Act Play Series; *Poe's Revenge on Shawn and Germaine: A Post-Hurricane Katrina Apocalyptic Tale*, produced as part of the Spontaneous Combustion Festival, No. 39, by Manhattan Theatre Source; and *Bassano and Shakespeare: No Love Story*, commissioned for production as part of the Amelia Plays Festival by the Dark Lady Players.

New York dramaturgical work includes *Comfort Women: A New Musical*, Theatre at Saint Clement's and concert engagement at Feinstein's/54 Below (www.comfortwomenmusical.com); *The Illusion of Love*, Planet Connections Theatre Festivity; SCCC One-Act Play Festival, Van Nostrand Theatre, Long Island, NY; *Out of Their Minds*, New Media Repertory Company; *Sex with the Censor and Other Plays by Theresa Rebeck*, TBG Theatre; *The Holy Cows of Credence, South Dakota: A New Moo-sical*, Planet Connections Theatre Festivity; and *Dream Deferred*, NuAfrikan Theatre Company at 133rd Street Arts Center, Harlem, NY.

An alumna of the University of Southern Maine (BA, theatre), Columbia University's School of the Arts (MFA, playwriting), and the Graduate Center, CUNY (MPhil and PhD, theatre), she is also a member of the Dramatists Guild of America. Potts co-founded (with Lydia Fort) and is managing director of Akademeia Theatre. In her day job, Dr. Potts is an assistant professor and has served as acting chair in the Theatre and Speech Department at the City College of New York, CUNY. With a passion for creating and teaching new courses for the twenty-first century, like Web Episode and Series Creation, she has received a Simon H. Rifkind Center for the Humanities Fellowship and an Excellence in Teaching Grant from the Michael J. Grant Campus, Suffolk County Community College, SUNY. Read her interview with Pulitzer Prize–winning playwright Quiara Alegría Hudes in *Guernica/A Magazine of Art and Politics* at https://www.guernica mag.com/interviews/water-by-the-spoonful.